THE UPWARD PATH

Daily inspirations from the Works of
Henry van Dyke

Harold Shaw Publishers
Wheaton, Illinois

Originally published as *The Friendly Year,* © 1887, 1893, 1898 by Henry van Dyke; 1889, 1891, 1892, 1897, 1898, 1895, 1897, 1898, 1899, 1900 by Charles Scribner's Sons; 1893, 1895, 1899 by Harper & Brothers; 1896, 1899 by the Macmillan Company; 1897, 1900 by T. Y. Crowell & Co.; 1900 by the Outlook Company

Copyright © 1995 by Harold Shaw Publishers

All rights reserved. No part of this book may be reproduced or transmitted in any form or by any means, electronic or mechanical, including photocopying, recording, or any information storage and retrieval system without written permission from Harold Shaw Publishers, Box 567, Wheaton, Illinois 60189. Printed in the United States of America.

ISBN 0-87788-249-5

Cover design by David LaPlaca

Edited by Lil Copan

Library of Congress Cataloging-in-Publication Data

Van Dyke, Henry, 1852-1933.
   [Friendly year]
   The upward path : daily inspirations from the works of Henry van Dyke.
      p. cm.
   Originally published: The friendly year. 1900.
   Includes bibliographical references.
   1. Devotional calendars. 2. Spiritual life—Christianity—Meditations. I. Title.
BV4832.V24 1995
242'.2—dc20   95-17800
                                                                  CIP

02 01 00 99 98 97 96 95

10 9 8 7 6 5 4 3 2 1

Editor's Preface

Mini-discussions on daily life, faith, nature, and art make Henry van Dyke's book a satisfying mix of readings. It is a pleasure to be able to bring van Dyke's warm-heartedness back into print.

In editing, we made changes that allow the reader a more focused blend of van Dyke's work. Most of the changes were insignificant: updating terms, using more inclusive language, editing for general clearness of ideas, and rearranging entries for purposes of layout. The slightly larger task was in taking out small sections of van Dyke's entries containing "chastened meliorism"—his belief that God's hand is visibly moving humanity toward improvement. Along with many theologians and philosophers in the time of the Industrial Revolution, van Dyke saw a parallel between whole-scale moral improvement and technological advance. This belief that everything was moving toward peaceful unity ran as a common current that lasted until the crushing entrance of the two world wars.

Van Dyke's essential work is here and remains clear in these pages. May these small entries give you the seeds of profound truths to take with you each day.

Bibliography

I. 1887. *The Story of the Psalms.* New York: Charles Scribner's Sons.

II. 1889. *The Poetry of Tennyson.* Tenth edition. New York: Charles Scribner's Sons.

III. 1893. *The Christ-Child in Art: A Study of Interpretation.* New York and London: Harper & Brothers.

IV. 1893. *Sermons to Young Men.* New York: Charles Scribner's Sons.

V. 1895. *The Story of the Other Wise Man.* New York and London: Harper & Brothers.

VI. 1895. *Little Rivers: A Book of Essays in Profitable Idleness.* New York: Charles Scribner's Sons.

VII. 1896. *The Gospel for an Age of Doubt.* New York: The Macmillan Company. London: Macmillan & Co., Ltd.

VIII. 1897. *Ships and Havens.* New York: Thomas Y. Crowell & Co.

IX. 1897. *The Builders and Other Poems.* New York: Charles Scribner's Sons.

X. 1897. *The First Christmas Tree: A Story of the Forest.* New York: Charles Scribner's Sons.

XI. 1898. *The Lost Word: A Christmas Legend of Long Ago.* New York: Charles Scribner's Sons.

XII. 1899. *The Gospel for a World of Sin: A Companion Volume to "The Gospel for an Age of Doubt."* New York: The Macmillan Company. London: Macmillan & Co., Ltd.

XIII. 1899. *Fisherman's Luck and Some Other Uncertain Things.* New York: Charles Scribner's Sons.

XIV. 1900. *The Toiling of Felix and Other Poems.* New York: Charles Scribner's Sons.

XV. 1900. *The Poetry of the Psalms: For Readers of the English Bible.* New York: Thomas Y. Crowell & Co.

The Roman numerals at the end of each selection will enable the reader to identify, by reference to the bibliographic list, the book from which it is taken. The Arabic numerals indicate the page on which the passage or stanza may be found.

The Upward Path

To be glad of life, because it gives you the chance to love and to work and to play and to look up at the stars; to be contented with your possessions, but not satisfied with yourself until you have made the best of them; to despise nothing in the world except falsehood and meanness, and to fear nothing except cowardice; to be governed by your admirations rather than by your disgusts; to covet nothing that is your neighbor's except his kindness of heart and gentleness of manners: to think seldom of your enemies, often of your friends, and every day of Christ; and to spend as much time as you can, with body and with spirit, in God's out-of-doors—these are little guideposts on the footpath to peace.

JANUARY

1. *The compass*

Four things a man must learn to do
If he would make his record true:
To think without confusion clearly;
To love his fellow men sincerely;
To act from honest motives purely;
To trust in God and heaven securely.
—*IX, 39.*

2. *White heather*

"Carry this little flower with you. It's not the bonniest blossom in Scotland, but it's the dearest, for the message that it brings. And you will remember that love is not getting, but giving; not a wild dream of pleasure, and a madness of desire—oh no, love is not that—it is goodness, and honor, and peace, and pure living—yes, love is that; and it is the best thing in the world, and the thing that lives longest. And that is what I am wishing for you and yours with this bit of white heather."
—*VI, 114.*

JANUARY

3. *The faith that steadies us*

Happy and strong and brave shall we be—able to endure all things, and to do all things—if we believe that every day, every hour, every moment of our life is in God's hands.
—*I, 154.*

4. *To a young woman*

TO

A YOUNG WOMAN

OF AN OLD FASHION

WHO LOVES ART

NOT FOR ITS OWN SAKE

BUT BECAUSE IT ENNOBLES LIFE

WHO READS POETRY

NOT TO KILL TIME

BUT TO FILL IT WITH BEAUTIFUL THOUGHTS

AND WHO STILL BELIEVES

IN GOD AND DUTY AND IMMORTAL LOVE

I DEDICATE

THIS BOOK

—*II, Dedication.*

JANUARY

5. Kinship

If I can feel sympathy—feel it within and without—then the dew falls and the desert begins to blossom. By sympathy I do not mean merely a fellowship in sorrow, but also, and no less truly, a fellowship in joy—a feeling for which we ought to have an English word. To be glad when your brothers and sisters are prosperous and happy, to rejoice in their success, to cheer for their victories; to be compassionate and pitiful when they are distressed and miserable, to grieve over their failures, to help them in their troubles—this is the fraternal spirit which blesses the one who exercises it, and those toward whom it is exercised.
—*I, 245.*

6. Epiphany

When our world learns this lesson; when pride bows down to meekness, and experience does homage to innocence—then the Epiphany will come, and a great light will lighten the nations.
—*III, 145.*

JANUARY

7. The minor parts

It is not required of every man and woman to be, or to do, something great; most of us must content ourselves with taking small parts in the chorus, as far as possible without discord. Shall we have no little lyrics because Homer and Dante have written epics? And because we have heard the great organ at Freiburg, shall the sound of Käthi's zither in the alpine hut please us no more? Even those who have greatness thrust upon them will do well to lay the burden down now and then, knowing that they are not altogether answerable for the conduct of the universe, or at least not all the time. "I reckon," said a cowboy to me one day, as we were riding through the Bad Lands of Dakota, "there's someone bigger than me running this outfit. He can 'tend to it well enough, while I smoke my pipe after the roundup."
—VI, 30.

8. The light that lifts us

Faith precedes repentance. Hope, not despair, is the mother of godly sorrow. The goodness of God is before the badness of man. The divine forgiveness antedates the human sin. It is not until we see the light shining above us that we begin to loathe our dark estate and receive strength to rise out of the gloom and climb upwards.
—I, 76.

JANUARY

9. A blossom-wonder

Only a little shrivelled seed,
It might be flower, or grass, or weed;
Only a box of earth on the edge
Of a narrow, dusty window ledge;
Only a few scant summer showers;
Only a few clear shining hours;
That was all. Yet God could make
Out of these, for a sick child's sake,
A blossom-wonder, as fair and sweet
As ever broke at an angel's feet.
—*IX, 41.*

10. Great and good things

It is only by thinking about great and good things that we come to love them, and it is only by loving them that we come to long for them, and it is only by longing for them that we are impelled to seek after them, and it is only by seeking after them that they become ours and we enter into vital experience of their beauty and blessedness.
—*IV, 74.*

JANUARY

11. Courage

There is no duty so small, no trial so slight, that it does not afford room for courage. It has a meaning and value for every phase of existence; for the workshop and for the battlefield, for the thronged city and for the lonely desert, for the sickroom and for the marketplace, for the study and for the counting house, for the church and for the drawing room. There is courage physical, and social, and moral, and intellectual—a soldier's courage, a doctor's courage, a lawyer's courage, a preacher's courage, a nurse's courage, a merchant's courage, a man's courage, a woman's courage—for courage is just strength of heart, and the strong heart makes itself felt everywhere, and lifts up the whole of life.
—*IV, 63.*

12. Discerning in part

In art all that is sincere and expressive and masterly is valuable. There is no school that has the monopoly of merit, no way of painting that is the only right way. In religion all that is pure and reverent and spiritual is precious. There is no exclusiveness in true piety or virtue. The thought of God is always "larger than the measure of man's mind," and each soul discerns but a fragment of it.
—*III, 108.*

JANUARY

13. *Plain living*

For the most part, our distress, our poverty, our foolish care come, not from the smallness of our provisions, but from the largeness of our pampered desires. We are afraid that we shall not always have cake, and so we forget that God has promised that his children shall not lack bread. We begin to put our foolish trust in gold, in clever enterprises, in wise investments, in daring speculations, because the things that we want are so numerous and so costly. A little plain living would lead to higher thinking.
—*I, 33.*

14. *The best joys of life*

It would do us good, it would do our children good, if we would learn that the real necessities and the best joys of human life are very simple, and for these we have a right always to trust God.
—*I, 33.*

15. *The pilgrimage*

All faith recognizes that life is a pilgrimage whose course and duration cannot be foreseen. That is true, indeed, whether we acknowledge it or not.
—*IV, 131.*

JANUARY

16. Joy and duty

"Joy is a duty"—so with golden lore
The Hebrew rabbis taught in days of yore,
And happy human hearts heard in
    their speech
Almost the highest wisdom man can reach.

But one bright peak still rises far above,
And there the Master stands whose name
    is Love,
Saying to those whom weary tasks employ:
"Life is divine when Duty is a Joy."
—*IX, 51.*

17. The spiritual character

The spiritual character is divinely ruled, submissive to a higher law, doing another will than its own, seeking the ends of virtue and holiness and unselfish love. It may have many inward struggles, many defeats, many bitter renunciations and regrets. It may appear far less peaceful, orderly, self-satisfied, than some of those who are secretly following the other ideal. Many a saint in the making seems to be marred by faults and conflicts from which the smug, careful, reputable sensualist is exempt. The difference between the two is not one of position. It is one of direction. The one, however high he stands, is moving down. The other, however low he starts, is moving up.
—*VIII, 32.*

JANUARY

18. *The divine escort*

God is present, also, in the dealings of his providence. If we trust him, he is guiding us by his counsel, he is defending us by his might, he is interposing to rescue us from our enemies. We are like ships sailing under the convoy of an invisible fleet; like pilgrims marching with an escort of countless armies; like a city guarded by unseen hosts of angels. God is not only *on* the side of his church and his people: he is *at* their side.
—I, 140.

19. *Forms and colors*

Silence. Solitude. The flocks noiselessly moving about him, the eagle sailing in slow circles above his head, the dawn struggling with night on the faraway hills, the dewdrops sparkling on the grass, the loud stream rushing through its rocky bed, the black shadows deepening in the narrow glen, the sheep gathering nearer to him and couching themselves in the twilight, the distant roar of the lion, the great stars sliding through the night, the trembling fugitive sharing his plain food as they looked down together from some safe eyrie upon the pastures below—these were the forms and colours of David's early life; and out of them he weaves a beautiful garment to clothe his thought of God.
—I, 31.

JANUARY

20. Wisdom versus wit

Epigrams are worth little for guidance to the perplexed, and less for comfort to the wounded. But the plain, homely sayings which come from a soul that has learned the lesson of patient courage in the school of real experience, fall upon the wound like drops of balsam, and like a soothing lotion upon the eyes smarting and blinded with passion.
—VI, 110.

21. Growing in glory

The strength of a wish depends upon the sincerity and earnestness and tenacity with which you fix your attention upon the things which are really great and worthy to be loved. This is what the apostle Paul means when he says, at the close of his description of a life which is strong, and inwardly renewed, and growing in glory even in the midst of affliction—"while we look not at the things which are seen, but at the things which are unseen." It is while we look that we learn to love. It is by loving that we learn to seek. And it is in seeking that we find and are blessed.
—IV, 75.

JANUARY

22. Cloud of witnesses

It may be that some saint dearer to you than any whose names are written among the Old Testament worthies—your own faithful mother, the father who prayed with you at the family altar, the friend who walked close beside you in the journey of life—is looking down upon you and watching your path today. And of this be sure: If you are following in the footsteps of Christ, if you are sacrificing yourself for others, if you are treading the path of duty and devotion, these are the things which they understand, and for which they bless and love you.
—*IV, 181.*

23. The life of the spirit

Vitality, in humans, is a spiritual force conditioned, but not created, by a material embodiment. A *vitometer* will never be invented, because there is no instrument delicate enough to take the temperature of the inner life. Even in dealing with bodily disease, the wise physician, while perhaps making the diagnosis absolute, always recognizes an element of uncertainty in the prognosis. "While there is life there is hope," the physician says, possibly adding, "While there is hope there is life." Hope has healed more diseases than any medicine.
—*XII, 91.*

JANUARY

24. The talk of friendship

But after all, the very best thing in good talk, and the thing that helps it most, is *friendship*. How it dissolves the barriers that divide us, and loosens all constraint, and diffuses itself like some fine old cordial through all the veins of life—this feeling that we understand and trust each other, and wish each other heartily well! Everything into which it really comes is good. It transforms letter writing from a task into a pleasure. It makes music a thousand times more sweet. The people who play and sing not *at* us, but *to* us—how delightful it is to listen to them! Yes, there is a talkability that can express itself even without words. There is an exchange of thought and feeling which is happy alike in speech and in silence. It is quietness pervaded with friendship.
—XII, 70.

25. Transforming uncertainty

Even if a person should fancy that their existence was secure, and that they could direct their own career and predict their own future, experience would teach them their mistake. But the point is that faith recognizes this uncertainty of life at the outset, and in a peculiar way, which transforms it from a curse into a blessing and makes it possible for us even to be glad that we must "go out not knowing whither we go."
—IV, 131.

JANUARY

26. *The open hand*

The open hand—not the blind eye nor the unfeeling heart, but the open hand—is the true symbol of God's dealing with mankind in the natural world. And this changes all, instantly and totally. Instead of the large indifference of Nature, we have the great beneficence of God. Instead of an unconscious mechanism, grinding out the same results and careless of the hands into which they fall, we have the wise and generous Father making ample and equal provision for all his children, bad and good.
—*IV, 198.*

27. *Manners*

It was a bare, rude place, but the dish of juicy trout was garnished with flowers, each fish holding a big pansy in its mouth, and as the woman set them down before me she wished me "a good appetite," with the hearty old-fashioned Tyrolese courtesy which still survives in these remote valleys. It is pleasant to travel in a land where the manners are plain and good. If you meet a peasant on the road he says, "God greet you!" If you give a child a couple of kreuzers he folds his hands and says, "God reward you!"
—*VI, 176.*

JANUARY

28. God's garden

Saints are God's flowers, fragrant souls
That His own hand hath planted,
Not in some far-off heavenly place,
Or solitude enchanted,
But here and there and everywhere,
In lonely field, or crowded town,
God sees a flower when He looks down.

Some wear the lily's stainless white,
And some the rose of passion,
And some the violet's heavenly blue,
But each in its own fashion,
With silent bloom and soft perfume,
Is praising Him who from above
Beholds each lifted face of love.
—IX, 49.

29. The wind and the rudder

Here is the sea on which you float, the sea of human life, with its shifting tides and currents. Yonder is the sky that bends above you, the pure and sovereign will of God. Out of that unsearchable heaven comes the breath of the Spirit, like "the wind that bloweth where it listeth, and thou canst not tell whence it cometh and whither it goeth." If you will spread your sail to catch that breath of life, if you will lay your course and keep your rudder true, you will be carried onward in peace and safety.
—IV, 221.

30. Shrunken miracles

Have we not all felt the shrinkage of the much-vaunted miracles of science into the veriest kitchen utensils of a comfort-worshipping society? Physical powers have been multiplied by an unknown quantity, but it is a serious question whether moral powers have not had their square root extracted.
—II, 288.

31. Woven on a Scottish loom

It is not half as far from Albany to Aberdeen as it is from New York to London. In fact, I venture to say that Americans on foot will find themselves less foreign in Scotland than in any other country in the Old World. There is something warm and hospitable—if the traveler knew the language well enough they would call it *couthy*—in the greeting gotten from the shepherd on the moor, and the conversation held with the farmer's wife in the stone cottage, where they stop to ask for a drink of milk and a bit of oatcake. The traveler feels that there must be a drop of Scotch somewhere in his mingled blood, or at least that the texture of his thought and feelings had been partly woven on a Scottish loom—perhaps the Westminster Shorter Catechism, or Robert Burns's poems, or the romances of Sir Walter Scott.
—VI, 93.

FEBRUARY

1. The step forward

We say that we "make up our minds" to do a certain thing or not to do it, to resist a certain temptation or to yield to it. It is true. We "make up our minds" in a deeper sense than we remember. In every case the ultimate decision is between two future selves, one with whom the virtue is harmonious, another with whom the vice is consistent. To one of these two figures, dimly concealed behind the action, we move forward. What we forget is, that, when the forward step is taken, the shadow will be *myself*.
—VII, 29.

2. Traveler's wisdom

Every country—or at least every country that is fit for habitation—has its own rivers; and every river has its own quality; and it is the part of wisdom to know and love as many as you can, seeing each in the fairest possible light, and receiving from each the best that it has to give.
—VI, 14.

FEBRUARY

3. Prayer: the strength of the weak

Prayer is the believer's comfort and support, weapon of defense, light in darkness, companionship in solitude, fountain in the desert, the believer's hope and deliverance.
—I, 193.

4. A choice in comrades

It is with rivers as it is with people: The greatest are not always the most agreeable nor the best to live with. The philosopher Diogenes must have been an uncomfortable bedfellow; the young companion Antinous was bored to death in the society of the Emperor Hadrian; and you can imagine much better company for a walking trip than Napoleon Bonapart; and in "the spacious times of great Elizabeth" there was many a milkmaid whom the wise man would have chosen for his friend, before the royal red-haired virgin.
—VI, 15.

5. Peace

With eager heart and will on fire,
I fought to win my great desire.
"Peace shall be mine," I said; but life
Grew bitter in the endless strife.

My soul was weary, and my pride
Was wounded deep: to Heaven I cried,
"God grant me peace or I must die."
The dumb stars glittered no reply.

Broken at last, I bowed my head,
Forgetting all myself, and said,
"Whatever comes, His will be done."
And in that moment peace was won.
—*IX, 53.*

6. The sweetness of surprise

A new door of happiness is opened when you go out to hunt for something and discover it with your own eyes. But there is an experience even better than that. When you have stupidly forgotten (or despondently foregone) to look about you for the unclaimed treasures and unearned blessings which are scattered along the byways of life; then, sometimes by a special mercy, a small sample of them is quietly laid before you so that you cannot help seeing it, and it brings you back, mighty sweetly, to a sense of the joyful possibilities of living.
—*XIII, 81.*

FEBRUARY

7. A verbal key

There is power in words, surely, and many a treasure besides Ali Baba's is unlocked with a verbal key. Some charm in the mere sound, some association with the pleasant past, touches a secret spring. The bars are down; the gate is open; you are made free of all the fields of memory and fancy—by a word.
—*VI, 183.*

8. Learning by doing

The word of Jesus in the mind of one who does not do the will of Jesus, lies like seed corn in a mummy's hand. It is only by dwelling with him and receiving his character, his personality so profoundly, so vitally that it shall be with us as if, in his own words, we had partaken of his flesh and his blood, as if his sacred humanity had been interwoven with the very fibers of our heart and pulsed with secret power in all our veins—it is thus only that we can be enabled to see his teaching as it is, and set it forth with luminous conviction to the souls of men.
—*VII, 201.*

FEBRUARY

9. Strength of heart

For every one of us, there is nothing more desirable, nothing more necessary, than real strength of heart. If we can obtain it from the divine and only source, it will make our lives straight and clean and fine. It will enable us to follow Jesus of Nazareth, who was not only the purest and gentlest, but also the bravest Spirit that ever dwelt on earth.
—*IV, 68.*

10. What is built into your house?

I wonder how often the inhabitant of the snug Queen Anne cottage in the suburbs remembers the picturesque toil and varied hardship that it has cost to hew and drag their walls and floors and pretty peaked roofs out of the backwoods. It might enlarge the home, and make the inhabitant's musings by the winter fireside less commonplace, to give a kindly thought now and then to the long chain of human workers through whose hands the timber of his house has passed, since it first felt the stroke of the axe in the snowbound winter woods, and floated, through the spring and summer, on far-off lakes and little rivers, *au large*.
—*VI, 220.*

FEBRUARY

11. The unseen world

Beyond our power of vision, poets say,
There is another world of forms unseen,
Yet visible to purer eyes than ours.
And if the crystal of our sight were clear,
We should behold the mountain slopes
    of cloud,
The moving meadows of the untilled sea,
The groves of twilight and the dales of dawn,
And every wide and lonely field of air,
More populous than cities, crowded close
With living creatures of all shapes and hues.
But if that sight were ours, the things
        that now
Engage our eyes would seem but dull
        and dim
Beside the splendors of our newfound world,
And we should be amazed and overwhelmed
Not knowing how to use the plenitude
Of vision.
   —*XIV, 46.*

FEBRUARY

12. Lincoln's birthday

Those who are raised high enough to be able to look over the stone walls, those who take a broader view of things than that which is bounded by the lines of any one state or section, understand that the unity of the nation is of the great importance, and are prepared to make those sacrifices and concessions, within the bounds of loyalty, which are necessary for its maintenance, and to cherish that temper of fraternal affection which can fill the form of national existence with the warm blood of life. The first man, after the civil war, to recognize this great principle and to act upon it was the head of the nation—that large and generous soul whose worth was not fully felt until he was taken from his people by the stroke of the assassin, in the very hour when his presence was most needed for the completion of the work of reunion.
—I, 240.

FEBRUARY

13. Secret safeguards

The grace of God—that secret influence of the Spirit of all good upon the hearts of men, which enables them to check their selfish passions, and draws them, even in spite of themselves, towards higher ideals; the power of religion—that deep sense of responsibility to a mightier and holier Being, and the apprehension of his judgment in another world; these are the influences which are chiefly operative in the preservation of civil order. They give dignity to law, and sanctity to government, and value to human life. If they were taken away, chaos would come.
—*I, 228.*

14. All the inventions

People can go from New York to London now in six days. But when they arrive they are not better people than if it had taken them a month. They can talk across three thousand miles of ocean, but they have nothing more to say than when they sent their letter by boat. All the inventions in the world will not change a person's heart, or "Lift him nearer [a] Godlike state."
—*II, 288.*

FEBRUARY

15. Entering into life

We are not saved through law; we are saved through life. Life does not mean outward obedience. That is only the shell of life. Real life means faith and hope and love. The only source of this life is in God. Christ alone brings this life near to us, makes it accessible, sweeps away all hindrances, and invites us to enter into it by giving ourselves entirely to him. To live, according to Paul, means to believe in Christ, to hope in Christ, and to love Christ, because he is the human life of God.
—*XII, 126.*

16. A treasure of life

If a king sent a golden cup full of cheering cordial to a weary person, they might well admire the twofold bounty of the royal gift. The beauty of the vessel would make the draught more gratifying and refreshing. And if the cup were inexhaustible, if it filled itself anew as often as it touched the lips, then the very shape and adornment of it would become significant and precious. It would be an inestimable possession, a singing goblet, a treasure of life.
—*XV, 6.*

FEBRUARY

17. Believe

Yes, I know you are trying to be good—fitfully, imperfectly, yet still trying. But there is something else that God would have you do first. He would have you believe that he wants you to be good, that he is willing to help you to be good, that he has sent his Son to make you good.
—IV, 49.

18. Meaningful greetings

I have often wished that every human employment might evolve its own appropriate greeting. Some of them would be peculiar, no doubt; but at least they would be an improvement on the wearisome iteration of "Good evening," and "Good morning," and the monotonous inquiry, "How do you do?"—a question so meaningless that it seldom tarries for an answer. Under the new and more natural system of etiquette, when you passed the time of day with a man you would know his business, and the salutations of the marketplace would be full of interest.
—XIII, 4.

FEBRUARY

19. *The reward of usefulness*

Wealth that comes as the reward of usefulness can be accepted with honor; and, consecrated to further usefulness, it becomes royal. Fame that comes from noble service, the gratitude of people, be they few or many, to one who has done them good, is true glory; and the influence that it brings is as near to godlike power as anything that man can attain. But whether these temporal rewards are bestowed upon us or not, the real desire of the soul is satisfied just in being useful. The pleasantest word that one can hear at the close of the day, whispered in secret to the soul, is "Well done, good and faithful servant!"
—*VIII, 27.*

20. *True heroes*

After all, have not the ones who win such a triumph as this in the hearts of the people, for whom they have made labor beautiful with the charm of art, deserved better of fame than many a crowned monarch or conquering warrior? We should be wiser if we gave less glory to those who have been successful in forcing their fellow human beings to die, and more glory to those who have been successful in teaching their fellow human beings how to live.
—*VI, 155.*

FEBRUARY

21. Implicit obedience

If we believe that this God is our God, and will be our guide even unto death, if we believe that this Christ is our only Savior and Master, our divine Leader and Guide, then we can go after him the more gladly just because he does not tell us all at once what we must resign and suffer and resist for his sake. That, indeed, might crush and dishearten us; for if we knew all at once, we could not help trying our strength against it all. But since we know only today's temptation, today's trial, today's conflict, today's cross, today; since we know that he who ordered it is with us and will help us to bear it, we can follow him in confidence.
—IV, 138.

22. Washington's birthday

Let a person fasten on to some great idea, some large truth, some noble cause, even in the affairs of this world, and it will send them forward with energy, with steadfastness, with confidence. This is what Emerson meant when he said, "Hitch your wagon to a star."
—IV, 42.

FEBRUARY

23. *The flame of patriotism*

Suppose it flashes upon you some day, as I believe it does flash upon most honest and high-minded people who read the history of their country, that all the hardships and perils and conflicts of the forebears—all the patient endurance of privations and the brave defiance of dangers, all the offerings of treasure and blood that have been made to found, liberate, defend, and preserve our country—are a price paid for you. Do you not see how that thought must kindle the flame of patriotism upon the altar of your heart?
—*IV, 111.*

24. *Eternal companionship*

The assurance of immortality alone is not enough. For if we are told that we are to live forever and still left without the knowledge of a personal God, eternity stretches before us like a boundless desert, a perpetual and desolate orphanage. It is a divine companionship that the spirit needs first of all and most deeply.
—*I, 165.*

25. Rendezvous

I count that friendship little worth
  Which has not many things untold,
  Great longings that no words can hold,
And passion-secrets waiting birth.

Along the slender wires of speech
  Some message from the heart is sent;
  But who can tell the whole that's meant?
Our dearest thoughts are out of reach.

I have not seen thee, though mine eyes
  Hold now the image of thy face;
  In vain, through form, I strive to trace
The soul I love: that deeper lies.

A thousand accidents control
  Our meeting here. Clasp hand in hand,
  And swear to meet me in that land
Where friends hold converse soul to soul.
—*IX, 40.*

26. Fire

Humans are the only creatures that dare to light a fire and to live with it. The reason? Because they alone have learned how to put it out.
—*XIII, 208.*

FEBRUARY

27. *The sure dwelling*

A tent for the wandering body, but an everlasting mansion for the believing soul—this is what Moses saw; this is what we can see when we take a long, true look at life. Wherever thou art, if thou believest in God, he is thy roof to shelter thee, he is thy hearth to warm thee, he is thy refuge and thy resting place. If once thou hast found this home and entered it, thou canst not be defenceless or forlorn, for he who remains the same amid all uncertainties and changes, he whose goodness antedates creation and whose faithfulness outwears the mountains, he with whom there is no variableness nor shadow of turning, is thy habitation and thy God.
—I, 18.

28. *The beginning of faith*

On the simplest soul that feels the wonder and the hidden glory of the universe, on the child to whom the stars are little windows into heaven, or the poet to whom "the meanest flower that blows can give / Thoughts that do often lie too deep for tears," God looks down with pleasure and approval. For in such a soul he sees the beginning of faith, which is able to pass behind the appearance to the reality, and make its possessor wise unto everlasting life.
—IV, 41.

FEBRUARY

29. *A different kind of joy*

One side of our nature, no doubt, finds its satisfaction in the regular, the proper, the conventional. But there is another side of our nature, underneath, that takes delight in the strange, the free, the spontaneous. We like to discover what we call a law of Nature, and make our calculations about it, and harness the force which lies behind it for our own purposes. But we taste a different kind of joy when an event occurs which nobody has foreseen or counted upon. It seems like an evidence that there is something in the world which is alive and mysterious and untrammelled.
—*XIII, 87.*

MARCH

1. *Lovers of liberty*

And thou, my country, write it on
    thy heart,
Thy sons are they who nobly take
    thy part;
Who dedicates his manhood at thy shrine,
Wherever born, is born a son of thine;
Foreign in name, but not in soul,
    they come
To find in thee their long-desired home;
Lovers of liberty and haters of disorder,
They shall be built in strength along
    thy border.
    —*IX, 82.*

2. *Interior joy*

This sacred joy is not to be a mere emotion stirring upon the surface of the life. It is to come from the heart as well as from the lips; it is to express a changed character, a new relation with God, a manner of life which sets itself in harmony with the divine will as noble words to noble music.
    —*I, 94.*

MARCH

3. "Bought with a price"

When we realize that every liberty, every privilege, every advantage, that comes to us as men and women has been bought with a price—that the dark, subterranean lives of those who toil day and night in the bowels of the earth, the perils and hardships of those who sail to and fro upon the stormy seas, the benumbing weariness of those who dig and ditch and handle dirt, the endless tending of looms and plying of needles and carrying of burdens—all this is done and endured and suffered by our fellow human beings, though blindly, for our benefit, and accrues to our advantage. When we begin to understand this, a nobler spirit enters into us, the only spirit that can keep our wealth, our freedom, our culture from being a curse to us forever, and sinking us into the ennui of a selfish hell.
—IV, 113.

4. A life of freedom

We desire our life to be a life of freedom, a life of noble service, a life of glad and happy labor for that which is highest and best. There is only one way to make it so, and that is to live it under the controlling power of the great price that has been paid for us.
—IV, 121

MARCH

5. *The noblest aim*

How simple and how beautiful is that phrase, "to please God." What a sense of nearness to the divine Being it gives us. What a noble statement of the true aim of life.
—*IV, 32.*

6. *Pleasing God*

There are a million ways of pleasing God, as many as the characters of men, as many as the hues and shades of virtue, as many as the conflicts between good and evil, as many as the calls to honest labor, as many as the opportunities of doing right and being good. That is the broad meaning of this eleventh chapter of the Hebrews, with its long roll of different achievements, with its list of men and women of every age, of every quality and condition, slaves and freemen, leaders and followers, warriors and statesmen, saints and sinners, silent martyrs, and nameless conquerors; there are a million ways of pleasing God, but not one without faith. Numberless forms of energy, but none without heat. Myriad colors of beauty, but none without light. All is cold and black until the sun shines. A universe of possibilities of goodness spreads before you, but not one of them can be realized unless you have faith. For without faith it is impossible to please God.
—*IV, 35.*

MARCH

7. Courage for the young

The stream chafes and frets through the rapids of the glen, and the river does not grow calm and smooth until it nears the sea. Courage is a virtue that the young cannot spare; to lose it is to grow old before the time; it is better to make a thousand mistakes and suffer a thousand reverses than to run away from the battle.
—VI, 111.

8. Courage for the old

Resignation is the courage of old age; it will grow in its own season; and it is a good day when it comes to us. Then there are no more disappointments; for we have learned that it is even better to desire the things that we have than to have the things that we desire.
—VI, 111.

9. Ever to hope

Just to give up, and rest
    All on a Love secure,
Out of a world that's hard at the best,
    Looking to heaven as sure;
Ever to hope, through cloud and fear,
In darkest night, that the dawn is near;
Just to wait at the Master's feet—
Surely, now, the bitter is sweet.
—IX, 63.

MARCH

10. *The standing army of the soul*

Genius is talent set on fire by courage. Fidelity is simply daring to be true in small things as well as great. As many as are the conflicts and perils and hardships of life, so many are the uses and the forms of courage. It is necessary, indeed, as the protector and defender of all the other virtues. Courage is the standing army of the soul which keeps it from conquest, pillage, and slavery.
—IV, 56.

11. *The lustre of the pearl*

He had taken from a secret resting place in his bosom the pearl, the last of his jewels. As he looked at it, a mellower luster, a soft and iridescent light, full of shifting gleams of azure and rose, trembled upon its surface. It seemed to have absorbed some reflection of the colors of the lost sapphire and ruby. So the profound, secret purpose of a noble life draws into itself the memories of past joy and past sorrow. All that has helped it, all that has hindered it, is transfused by a subtle power into its very essence. It becomes more luminous and precious the longer it is carried close to the warmth of the beating heart.
—V, 58.

MARCH

12. *The ransom*

This was the third trial, the ultimate probation, the final and irrevocable choice.

Was it his great opportunity, or his last temptation? He could not tell. One thing only was clear in the darkness of his mind—it was inevitable. And does not the inevitable come from God?

One thing only was sure to his divided heart—to rescue this helpless girl would be a true deed of love. And is not the love the light of the soul?

He took the pearl from his bosom. Never had it seemed so luminous, so radiant, so full of tender, living luster. He laid it in the hand of the slave.

"This is thy ransom, daughter! It is the last of my treasures which I kept for the king."
—*V, 66.*

13. *A better wisdom*

It is not until the soul has learned a better wisdom, learned that the human race is one, and that none can really rise by treading on fellow human beings, learned that true art is not the slave of luxury, but the servant of humanity, learned that happiness is born, not of the lust to possess and enjoy, but of the desire to give and to bless—then, and not until then, when she brings others with her, can the soul find true rest.
—*II, 45.*

14. Public spirit

The best way to show public spirit is by cultivating the private virtues. The first thing that you can do for your city is, to make a pure and sunny and healthful home in it; and the second thing is like unto the first, to help and encourage others to do the same. If you will honestly try to do this, you will find that you need, and you certainly will receive, the blessing of the Lord out of Zion.
—*I, 231.*

15. The Father's wish

I was talking not long ago with a man of business whose career had been full of large financial triumphs, but the one fact on which he seemed to dwell with most satisfaction was that his daughter had often said to him, "You have been a good father to me." She had blessed him; and that was what he most desired.

Not otherwise is it with God. When he calls himself our Father, he means not only that he is good to us, but also that he wishes and seeks our answering love. He would see his benevolence reflected in our gratitude, as the sunlight is given back from the surface of the lake. He would have our benediction. When we speak well of him, when we acknowledge his goodness and express our desire for his glory, he is well pleased.
—*I, 254.*

16. Contrasts

If all the skies were sunshine,
    Our faces would be fain
To feel once more upon them
    The cooling plash of rain.

If all the world were music,
    Our hearts would often long
For one sweet strain of silence,
    To break the endless song.

If life were always merry,
    Our souls would seek relief,
And rest from weary laughter
    In the quiet arms of grief.
    —IX, 16.

17. The other side of mercy

I am no friend to the people who receive the bounties of Providence without visible gratitude. When the sixpence falls into your hat, you may laugh. When the messenger of an unexpected blessing takes you by the hand and lifts you up and bids you walk, you may leap and run and sing for joy, even as the lame man, whom St. Peter healed, skipped piously and rejoiced aloud as he passed through the Beautiful Gate of the Temple. There is no virtue in solemn indifference. Joy is just as much a duty as beneficence is. Thankfulness is the other side of mercy.
    —XIII, 26.

MARCH

18. The quest

"My son, it may be that the light of truth is in this sign that has appeared in the skies, and then it will surely lead to the Prince and the mighty brightness. Or it may be that it is only a shadow of the light, as the king Tigranes has said, and then he who follows it will have only a long pilgrimage and an empty search. But it is better to follow even the shadow of the best than to remain content with the worst. And those who would see wonderful things must often be ready to travel alone. I am too old for this journey, but my heart shall be a companion of the pilgrimage day and night, and I shall know the end of thy quest. Go in peace."
—V, 19.

19. What money cannot buy

It is not true that a person can dispose of money *as they choose*. The purposes for which it can be used are strictly bounded. There are many things that one cannot buy with it; for example, health, long life, wisdom, a cheerful spirit, a clear conscience, peace of mind, a contented heart.

You never see the stock called Happiness quoted on the exchange. How high would it range, think you—a hundred shares of Happiness Preferred, guaranteed 7%, seller 30?
—VIII, 20.

MARCH

20. *The seeds of trouble*

Life is a troubled dream. It does not flow smoothly. It has moments of distress and fear. And the cause of its disturbance is our secret sin which God sets in the light of his countenance. Our physical transgression against the laws of our well-being, which bear their fruits in aches and pains and infirmities; our spiritual transgressions, the evil passions of anger and envy and lust, which we have harbored in our hearts until they have filled us with conflict and discontent; all those faults and follies of which we in our blindness were ignorant, but which the all-wise God could not help seeing, have sown the seeds of trouble, and we have reaped the harvest of grief.
—*I, 20.*

21. *Every gleam of beauty*

There are a hundred touches of kindness that come to us every day to tell us that we are not orphans or outcasts upon the earth. Every trace of order, every gleam of beauty, every provision of bounty in the natural world, is an evidence that it is God's house.
—*I, 35.*

MARCH

22. The companionable river

A river is the most human and companionable of all inanimate things. It has a life, a character, a voice of its own, and is as full of good fellowship as a sugar maple is of sap. It can talk in various tones, loud or low, and of many subjects, grave and gala. Under favorable circumstances it will even make a shift to sing, not in a fashion that can be reduced to notes and set down in black and white on a sheet of paper, but in a vague, refreshing manner, and to a wandering air.

For real company and friendship, there is nothing outside of the animal kingdom that is comparable to a river.
—VI, 9.

23. The peace of being in place

As living beings we are part of a universe of life; as intelligent beings we are in connection with a great circle of conscious intelligences; as spiritual beings we have our place in a moral world controlled and governed by the supreme Spirit. In each of these spheres there is a law, a duty, an obligation, a responsibility, for us. And our felicity lies in the discovery and acknowledgment of those ties which fit us and bind us to take our place, to play our part, to do our work, to live our life, where we belong.
—IV, 104.

MARCH

24. *Memory's choice*

Memory is a capricious and arbitrary creature. You never can tell what pebble she will pick up from the shore of life to keep among her treasures, or what inconspicuous flower of the field she will preserve as the symbol of "Thoughts that do often lie too deep for tears." She has her own scale of values for these mementos, and knows nothing of the market price of precious stones or the costly splendor of rare orchids. The thing that pleases her is the thing that she will hold fast. And yet I do not doubt that the most important things are always the best remembered; only we must learn that the real importance of what we see and hear in the world is to be measured at last by its meaning, its significance, its intimacy with the heart of our heart and the life of our life.
—VI, 104.

25. *The way*

Who seeks for heaven alone to save his soul,
May keep the path, but will not reach
    the goal;
While he who walks in Love may wander far,
But God will bring him where the
    Blessed are.
—IX, 64.

MARCH

26. *The key of the heart*

Wondrous power of music! How often has it brought peace, and help, and strength to weary and downcast pilgrims! It penetrates the bosom and unlocks the doors of secret, silent, self-consuming anguish, so that the sorrow flowing out may leave the soul unburdened and released. It touches the chords of memory, and the cadence of old songs brings back the happy scenes of the past. In the rude mining camp, cut off by the snows of winter, in the narrow cabin of the ship icebound in Arctic seas, in the bare, dark rooms of Libby prison where the captive soldiers are trying to beguile the heavy time in company, tears steal down the rough cheeks, and voices quaver with half pain, half pleasure, when someone strikes up familiar notes.

—I, 163.

27. *Feeble lives*

Is there any reason why our lives should be feeble and stagnant and worthless? Is there any reason why we should not overcome temptation and endure trial, and work the works of God in the world, and come at last to the height of his abode in heaven? Only one—that we do not know him who is able to do exceedingly abundantly above all that we ask or think, according to the power that worketh in us.

—IV, 96.

28. New life

Acknowledge the Lord Jesus as your Savior, Owner, Master, King. Confess the greatness of your obligation to him. Confess that you can never repay it. And then give yourself to him to live as bravely, as purely, as faithfully, as nobly as you can in his name and for his sake.
—*IV, 121.*

29. A tree with deep roots

Trees seem to come close to our life. They are often rooted in our richest feelings, and our sweetest memories, like birds, build nests in their branches. I remember the last time that I saw James Russell Lowell (only a few weeks before his musical voice was hushed). He walked out with me into the quiet garden at Elmwood to say good-by. There was a great horse chestnut tree beside the house, towering above the gable, and covered with blossoms from base to summit—a pyramid of green supporting a thousand smaller pyramids of white. The poet looked up at it with his gray, pain-furrowed face, and laid his trembling hand upon the trunk. "I planted the nut," said he, "from which this tree grew. And my father was with me and showed me how to plant it."
—*VI, 10.*

MARCH

30. Wayward weather

The weather forecaster tells us of an approaching storm. It comes according to the program. We admire the accuracy of the prediction, and congratulate ourselves that we have such a good meteorological service. But when, perchance, a bright, crystalline piece of weather arrives instead of the foretold tempest, do we not feel a secret sense of pleasure which goes beyond our mere comfort in the sunshine? The whole affair is not as easy as a sum in simple addition, after all—at least not with our present knowledge. It is a good joke on the Weather Bureau. "Aha, Old Probabilities!" we say. "You don't know it all yet; there are still some chances to be taken!"
—*XIII, 87.*

31. Truth in art

An idea arrives without effort; a form can only be wrought out by patient labor. If your story is worth telling, you ought to love it enough to be willing to work over it until it is true—true not only to the ideal, but true also to the real. The light is a gift; but the local color can only be seen by one who looks for it long and steadily.
—*V, xii.*

APRIL

1. The journey's course

The course of our journey has been appointed by God; he knows the way even through the darkness, and its goal is in his bosom. Be of good cheer; your Shepherd has overcome the world.
—I, 34.

2. Our sun

For the Lord God is our sun, and while he shines the world is bright.
—I, 52.

3. Concord

The cottage, no less than the palace, enjoys the blessings of civil concord and social harmony. Human life, in every sphere, becomes easier and happier and more fruitful, as people recognize the ties which bind them to each other, and learn to dwell together in mutual affection and helpfulness.
—I, 245.

APRIL

4. The testimony of gladness

An exclamation is often better than a description; a song is often more instructive than a sermon; and David could not have proved or explained the reality of his repentance in any other way so well as by this quick and joyous outburst of music. It is like the gleam of rosy light upon the western Alps; when we see it we know that the sun has risen. It is like an involuntary echo from the heart; when we hear it we know that God has spoken the word of peace. I had rather see a pardoned sinner show his happiness than hear him define his experience.
—I, 89.

5. Absorbed in loving obedience

We cannot have happiness until we forget to seek for it. We cannot find peace until we enter the path of self-sacrificing usefulness. We cannot be delivered from this "vain expense of passions that forever ebb and flow," this wretched, torturing, unsatisfied, unsatisfying self, until we come to Jesus and give our lives to him to be absorbed as his life was in loving obedience to God and loving service to our fellow human beings.
—IV, 165.

APRIL

6. Heaven within

Pain, disgrace, disaster, even the literal pangs of fire, we might endure. For an outward hell could not burn one whose heart had been cleansed, whose spirit had been renewed. Such a spirit would carry the water of life and the singing angels and the golden city and the eternal blessedness within itself, and there is not a corner of this wide universe where it could be really cast away from the presence of God. Let us not pray chiefly that God would let us into heaven, but first that he would send heaven into us.

> "Restore unto me the joy of thy salvation,
> And uphold me with a free spirit."
> —I, 81.

7. Gratitude

"Yes," she answered, lifting her eyes to his face; "I, too, have felt it: this burden, this need, this unsatisfied longing. I think I know what it means. It is gratitude—the language of the heart, the music of happiness. There is no perfect joy without gratitude. But we have never learned it, and the want of it troubles us. It is like being dumb with a heart full of love. We must find the word for it, and say it together. Then we shall be perfectly joined in perfect joy."
—XI, 47.

APRIL

8. The cross

The cross speaks silently but surely of God's great love for sinners. For this reason it has become the sign under which Christianity has won its way in a world of sin. This is not a theory of theology. It is a fact of history. Wherever the religion of Christ has advanced, its song of victory has been the burden of the ancient Latin hymn:

> "Forward the royal banners fly,
> The sacred cross shines out on high,
> Where man's Creator stooped to die
> In human flesh, to draw man nigh."

The same burden is repeated in the later music of the modern church:

> "Onward, Christian soldiers,
>   Marching as to war,
> With the cross of Jesus
>   Going on before."
> —XII, 171.

9. Power

No one in the world today has such power as they who can make their fellow human beings feel that Christ is a reality.
—IV, 244.

APRIL

10. *By faith*

Lay hold on him by faith and all things are possible. Let us clasp the hand of Christ and climb; and as we climb he will lift us out of sin, out of selfishness, out of weakness, out of death, into holiness, into love, into strength, into life, and we shall know the power of his resurrection.
—IV, 96.

11. *Arise and follow*

Self is the only prison that can ever bind
    the soul;
Love is the only angel who can bid the
    gates unroll:
And when he comes to call thee, arise and
    follow fast;
His way may lie through darkness, but it
    leads to light at last.
—IX, 48.

12. *Living evidence*

A poem like Tennyson's *In Memoriam*, more than all flowers of the returning spring, more than all shining wings that flutter above the ruins of the chrysalis, more than all sculptured tombs and monuments of the beloved dead, is the living evidence and intimation of an endless life.
—II, 150.

APRIL

13. Preparing to travel

And is not the best of all our hopes—the hope of immortality—always before us? How can we be dull or heavy while we have that new experience to look forward to? It will be the most joyful of all our travels and adventures. It will bring us our best acquaintances and friendships.
—VI, 112.

14. The kingdom of heaven

In heaven the divine will is unopposed, and therefore the empire of heaven is peace and holiness and unbroken love. On earth the divine will is opposed and resisted, and therefore earth is a scene of conflict and sin and discord. For this reason the kingdom of heaven must *come* to earth, it must win its way, it must strive with the kingdom of darkness and overcome it. God's sovereignty in heaven is triumphant. God's sovereignty on earth is militant, in order that it may triumph—and triumph not in universal destruction, but in the salvation of all who will submit to it and embrace it and work with it—triumph, not by bare force, as gravitation triumphs over stones, but by holy love, as fatherly wisdom and affection triumph over the reluctance and rebellion of wayward children.
—VII, 268.

APRIL

15. The purifying hope

This is what the apostle means by "the power of an endless life." The passion of immortality is the thing that immortalizes our being. To be in love with heaven is the surest way to be fitted for it. Desire is the magnetic force of character. Character is the compass of life. "He that hath this hope in him purifieth himself."
—*VIII, 36.*

16. The mark of the King

Read the roll of those in every age whom the world has acknowledged as the best Christians—kings and warriors and philosophers, martyrs and heroes and laborers in every noble cause, the purest and the highest of mankind—and you will see that the test by which they are judged, the mark by which they are recognized, is likeness and loyalty to the personal Christ. Then turn to the work which the church is doing today in the lowest and darkest fields of human life, among the submerged classes of our great cities, among the sunken races of heathendom, and you cannot deny that the force of that work to enlighten and uplift, still depends upon the simplicity and reality with which it reveals the person of Jesus to the hearts of individuals.
—*VII, 66.*

APRIL

17. *The music in the tumult*

Even the broken and tumultuous noise
That rises from great cities, where the heart
Of human toil is beating heavily
With ceaseless murmurs of the
    laboring pulse,
Is not a discord; for it speaks to life
Of life unfeigned, and full of hopes and fears,
And touched through all the trouble of
    its notes
With something real and therefore glorious.
—*XIV, 40.*

18. *Household piety*

Surely it would be a good thing, if, in our schools, it could be recognized that a child would far better grow up thinking that the earth is flat, than to remain ignorant of God and moral law and filial duty. And it would be a still better thing, if, in all our homes, there could be a sincere revival of household piety—piety in the old Roman sense, which means the affectionate reverence of children for parents; piety in the new Christian sense which means the consecration to the heart of God—for this would rekindle the flame of devotion upon many a neglected altar, and shed a mild and gracious light through many a gloomy home, making it the brightest, cheerfulest, holiest place on earth.
—*I, 230.*

APRIL

19. Prayers without words

But if there were Someone above the moon and stars who did know and care, Someone who could see the places and the people that you and I would give so much to see, Someone who could do for them all of kindness that you and I fain would do, Someone able to keep our beloved in perfect peace and watch over the little children sleeping in their beds beyond the sea—what then? Why, then, in the evening hour, one might have thoughts of home that would go across the ocean by way of heaven, and be better than dreams, almost as good as prayers.
—VI, 243.

20. Jesus and the children

It is the religion of Jesus that has transfigured martyrdom and canonized innocence. It is the religion of Jesus that tells us of a heaven full of children, and a kingdom which is to bring heaven down to earth. And so long as the religion of Jesus lives, it will mean help and blessing to the martyred innocents of our race—the children who are oppressed in slavery, and neglected in want, and crushed by human avarice and ambition and cruelty in the wheels of the great world—help and blessing to these little ones in the name and for the sake of Jesus.
—III, 186.

APRIL

21. *Faith*

In the sphere of knowledge, in the sphere of action, in the sphere of character, faith is the one element that gives life and power to please God.
—*IV, 38.*

22. *"As a dream when one awaketh"*

Life is a dream. While we are in it, it seems to be long and full of matter. But when it draws to an end, we realize that it has passed while the clock was striking on the wall. "As I look back," says the old man, "it seems to me but yesterday that I first knew I was alive."
—*I, 20.*

23. *A living soul*

When a person can willingly forego even the outward services of religion, and stay away from the house of God, and let the seasons of devotion and communion pass by without a thought of regret, that person's faith and love must be at a low ebb, if indeed they have not altogether dried up and blown away. A living plant seeks water: a living soul longs for the refreshment of the sanctuary.
—*I, 107.*

APRIL

24. *The liberty of little rivers*

It is not only to the real life of birds and flowers that little rivers introduce you. They lead you often into familiarity with human nature in undress, rejoicing in the liberty of old clothes, or of none at all. People do not mince along the banks of streams in patent leather shoes or crepitating silks. Corduroy and homespun and flannel are the stuffs that suit this region; and the frequenters of these paths go their natural gaits, in calfskin or rubber boots, or barefooted. The girdle of conventionality is laid aside, and the skirts rise with the spirits.
—*VI, 25.*

25. *Deeper understanding*

We may be able to tell how many stars are in the Milky Way; we may be able to count the petals of every flower, and number the bones of every bird; but unless faith leads us to a deeper understanding, a more reverent comprehension of the significance of the universe, God can no more be pleased with our knowledge than the painter is pleased with the fly which touches his picture with its feelers, and sips the varnish from the surface, and dies without dreaming of the meaning, thought, feeling, embodied in the colors.
—*IV, 41.*

APRIL

26. Wings of a dove

I

At sunset, when the rosy light was dying
    Far down the pathway of the west,
I saw a lonely dove in silence flying,
        To be at rest.

Pilgrim of air, I cried, could I but borrow
    Thy wandering wings, thy freedom blest,
I'd fly away from every careful sorrow,
        And find my rest.

II

But when the dusk a filmy veil was weaving,
    Back came the dove to seek her nest
Deep in the forest where her mate was
    grieving—
        There was true rest.

Peace, heart of mine! no longer sigh to
    wander;
    Lose not thy life in fruitless quest.
There are no happy islands over yonder;
        Come home and rest.
—*IX, 3.*

APRIL

27. Taking ourselves too seriously

There is such a thing as taking ourselves and the world too seriously, or at any rate too anxiously. Half of the secular unrest and dismal, profane sadness of modern society comes from the vain idea that every person is bound to be a critic of life, and to let no day pass without finding some fault with the general order of things, or projecting some plan for its improvement. And the other half comes from the greedy notion that life does consist, after all, in the abundance of the things that one possesses, and that it is somehow or other more respectable and pious to be always at work making a larger living, than it is to lie on your back in the green pastures and beside the still waters, and thank God that you are alive.
—VI, 30.

28. Our triumphs and joys

It does not matter so much, after all, what happens to us, whether we are obscured or honored, whether we are praised or condemned, whether we are lifted up or cast down, provided only we can see God rising above the horizon, and filling not the heaven alone, but also the earth, with his glory. The triumph of his truth, the spread of his gospel, the victory of his redeeming love over the darkness of sin—these are our triumphs and joys.
—I, 52.

29. A divine ambition

To please God, the perfect, radiant Being, the most wise, the most holy, the most beautiful, the most loving of all spirits; to perform some task, achieve some victory, bring some offering that shall be acceptable to him, and in which he shall delight; simply to live our life, whatever it may be, so that he, the good and glorious God, shall approve and bless it, and say of it, "Well done," and welcome it into the sense of his own joy—that is a divine ambition. "What vaster dream could hit the mood / Of love on earth?"
—*IV, 34.*

30. Never harmed

Do we not know that more than half our trouble is borrowed? Just suppose that we could get rid of all unnecessary and previous terror; just suppose that we could be sure of final victory in every conflict, and final emergence out of every shadow into brighter day; how our hearts would be lightened, how much more bravely we should work and fight and march forward! This is the courage to which we are entitled and which we may find in the thought that God is with us everywhere. He will not let anyone destroy us. We may be hurt, but we can never be harmed.
—*I, 34.*

MAY

1. The echo in the heart

It's little I can tell
   About the birds in books;
And yet I know them well,
   By their music and their looks:
      When May comes down the lane,
      Her airy lovers throng
      To welcome her with song,
      And follow in her train:
      Each minstrel weaves his part
      In that wildflowery strain,
      And I know them all again
      By their echo in my heart.
—*XIV, 73.*

2. Boundary line of knowledge

Do you remember what Moses saw on the mount? He said unto the Lord, "I beseech thee show me thy glory." But God answered, "I will make all my goodness pass before thee." Here is the boundary line of knowledge: God's goodness is revealed; but his glory is beyond the horizon.
—*IV, 219.*

MAY

3. *The oldest game*

There is a secret pleasure in finding delicate flowers in the rough heart of the wilderness. It is like discovering the veins of poetry in the character of a guide or a lumberjack. And to be able to call the plants by name makes them a hundredfold more sweet and intimate.

Naming things is one of the oldest and simplest of human pastimes. Children play at it with their dolls and toy animals. In fact, it was the first game ever played on earth, for the Creator who planted the garden eastward in Eden knew well what would please the childish heart of man, when he brought all the new-made creatures to Adam, "to see what he would call them."
—VI, 260.

4. *When all things speak*

God is present with his own people in a sense which belongs to them alone. He is present by the revelations of his glory. They have learned to see his face and hear his voice in the world, so that the stars, which to others are silent, speak of his wisdom to every faithful heart, and the sea tells of his power, and the fruits and flowers of earth seem to those who love him as if they were offered by his bountiful hands.
—I, 139.

MAY

5. Forgiveness

This world is too sweet and fair to darken it with the clouds of anger. This life is too short and precious to waste it in bearing that heaviest of all burdens, a grudge. Forgive and forget if you can; but *forgive* anyway; and pray heartily and kindly for all people, for thus only shall we be the children of our Father who maketh his sun to rise on the evil and the good, and sendeth rain on the just and on the unjust.
—*IV, 210.*

6. A full life

If your cup is small, fill it to the brim. Let it be *multum in parvo*. Make the most of your opportunities of honest work and pure pleasure. If we had twice as much time to spend, we could not afford to squander any of it on vain regrets, or anxious worriments, or idle reveries. The best thing that we can get is what the text calls "a heart of wisdom"; for such a heart is full of medicine for the day of sickness, and music for the day of sadness, and strength for the day of trial, and riches for eternity. Remember that what you possess in the world will be found at the day of your death to belong to someone else; but what you are, will be yours forever.
—*I, 22.*

MAY

7. Be not silent

A silent love is acceptable only from the lower animals. God has given us speech that we should call upon his name. Worship is to religion what fragrance is to the flower.
—I, 256.

8. The pathos of beauty

How the heart expands at such a view! Nine miles of shining water lay stretched before us, opening through the mountains that guarded it on both sides with lofty walls of green and gray, ridge over ridge, point beyond point, until the vista ended in "yon orange sunset waning slow."

At a moment like this one feels a sense of exultation. It is a new discovery of the joy of living. And yet, my friend and I confessed to each other there was a tinge of sadness, an inexplicable regret mingled with our joy. Was it the thought of how few human eyes had ever seen that lovely vision? Was it the dim foreboding that we might never see it again? Who can explain that secret pathos of Nature's loveliness? It is a touch of melancholy inherited from our mother Eve. It is an unconscious memory of the lost Paradise. It is the sense that even if we should find another Eden, we would not be fit to enjoy it perfectly, nor stay in it forever.
—VI, 210.

MAY

9. The voices

The evil voices in the souls of men,
Voices of rage and cruelty and fear
Have not dismayed me; for I have perceived
The voices of the good, the kind, the true
    excel in strength.
—*XIV, 50.*

10. Courage

Many people are so afraid to die that they have never begun to live. But courage emancipates us and gives us to ourselves, that we may give ourselves freely and without fear to God.
—*IV, 58.*

11. The cause

Often does it happen that people who are engaged in the noblest work need to be reminded that the cause for which they are laboring is holier than themselves.
—*I, 60.*

MAY

12. Wildflowers

For my own part, I approve of garden flowers because they are so orderly and so certain; but wildflowers I love, just because there is so much chance about them. Nature is all in favor of certainty in great laws and and of uncertainty in small events. You cannot appoint the day and the place for her flower shows. If you happen to drop in at the right moment she will give you a free admission. But even then it seems as if the table of beauty had been spread for the joy of a higher visitor, and in obedience to secret orders which you have not heard.
—*XIII, 83.*

13. The speech of the seasons

If people would only hear it! Oh that the deaf ear and the dull heart might be touched and opened to the beautiful speech of the seasons, so that plenty might draw all souls to gratitude, and beauty move all spirits to worship, and every fair landscape, and every overflowing harvest, and every touch of loveliness and grace upon the face of the world, might lift all souls that live and feel from Nature up to Nature's God! This is what he longs for. This is what he means when he tells us, in his impartial sunshine and rain, that he is the Father of all.
—*IV, 201.*

MAY

14. The hill of sighs

We are often standing upon the hill of sighs, and looking back to the pleasant places which our feet shall tread no more, recalling the opportunities which have departed, remembering the sweet Sabbaths in the home of childhood, the mornings when we went with the multitude of friends to the house of God, the quiet evenings filled with the voice of sacred song, the days when it seemed easy and natural to be good, when gracious currents of holy influence were bearing us onward, almost without effort, towards a better life.
—*I, 167.*

15. Luminous evidences of a divine word

The Bible, if indeed it be the true textbook of religion, must contain the answer to a person's cry as a sinner to God as Savior. It must disclose to humanity a remedy for the pain, a consolation for the shame, a rescue from the fear, and a confirmation of the secret hope, that they dimly and confusedly feel in the sense of sin. A Bible with no message of deliverance from sin would be a useless luxury in a sinful world. It would lack that quality of perfect fitness to human need which is one of the most luminous evidences of a divine word. The presence of a clear message of salvation is an essential element in the proof of inspiration.
—*XII, 51.*

16. Mutual blessing

In our own tongue the word *bless* is derived from the same root as *blithe* and *bliss*. It conveys the thought of peace and happiness. When we bless God we express the sincere desire that, as the source of all light and life, as the maker and ruler of the universe, his glory may shine everywhere, and that all his works may praise him in all places of his dominion. When God blesses us, he promises to satisfy our souls.
—I, 250.

17. Chance

"Chance" is a disreputable word, I know. It is supposed by many pious persons to be improper and almost blasphemous to use it. But I am not one of those who share this verbal prejudice. I am inclined rather to believe that it is a good word to which a bad reputation has been given. For what does it mean, after all, but that some things happen in a certain way which might have happened in another way? Where is the immorality, the irreverence, the atheism in such a supposition? Certainly God must be competent to govern a world in which there are possibilities of various kinds, just as well as one in which every event is inevitably determined beforehand.
—XIII, II.

18. The life that counts

Never has there been a time when character and conduct counted for more than they do today. A life on a high level, yet full of helpful, healing sympathy for all life on its lowest levels, is the first debt we owe to our fellow human beings in this age.
—VII, 43.

19. The uncertainty of life

People who have faith accept the uncertainty of life as the consequence of its larger significance; they cannot interpret it, because it means so much; they cannot trace its lines through to the end, because it has no end, it runs on into God's eternity. Something better is coming into it than worldly success. Something better is coming out of it than wealth or fame or power. They are not making themselves. God is making them, and that after a model which eye hath not seen, but which is to be manifest in the consummation of the children of God. So they can toil away at work, not knowing whether they are to see its result now or not, but knowing that God will not let it be wasted. So they can run with patience the race that is set before them, not knowing whether they shall come in first or last among fellow human beings, but knowing that the prize is secure.
—IV, 133.

MAY

20. *The power that fails not*

Was it long ago, or was it but yesterday, that we prayed for strength to perform a certain duty, to bear a certain burden, to overcome a certain temptation, and received it? Do we dream that the divine force was exhausted in answering that one prayer? No more than the great river is exhausted by turning the wheels of one mill. Put it to the proof again with today's duty, today's burden, today's temptation. Thrust yourself further and deeper into the stream of God's power, and feel it again, as you have felt it before, able to do exceedingly abundantly. Remember and trust.
—*IV, 88.*

21. *The flower and the seed*

Where you find a flower, you know there must have been a seed. Where you find a river, you know there must be a spring. Where you see a flame, you know there must be a fire. Where you find a person beloved and blessed of God, you know there must be faith. Whether it is recorded or not, whether you can see it or not, it must be there, germ of this person's virtue, fountainhead of their goodness, living source of warmth and light; for without faith it is impossible to please God.
—*IV, 31.*

MAY

22. *The work that endures*

We long to leave something behind us which shall last, some influence of good which shall be transmitted through our children, some impress of character or action which shall endure and perpetuate itself. There is only one way in which we can do this, only one way in which our lives can receive any lasting beauty and dignity; and that is by being taken up into the great plan of God. Then the fragments of broken glass glow with an immortal meaning in the design of his grand mosaic. Then our work is established, because it becomes part of his work.
—I, 23.

23. *Spiritual power*

The vision of spiritual power, even as we see it in the imperfect manifestations of human life, is ennobling and uplifting. The rush of courage along the perilous path of duty is finer than the foaming leap of the torrent from the crag. Integrity resisting temptation overtops the mountains in grandeur. Love, giving and blessing without limit, has a beauty and a potency of which the sunlight is but a faint and feeble image. When we see these things they thrill us with joy; they enlarge and enrich our souls.
—IV, 80.

MAY

24. A nameless charm

Little rivers seem to have the indefinable quality that belongs to certain people in the world—the power of drawing attention without courting it, the faculty of exciting interest by their very presence and way of doing things.
—*VI, 19.*

25. Fatherhood

The boy enjoyed this kind of father at the time, and later he came to understand, with a grateful heart, that there is no richer inheritance in all the treasury of unearned blessings. For, after all, the love, the patience, the kindly wisdom of a grown man who can enter into the perplexities and turbulent impulses of a boy's heart, and give him cheerful companionship, and lead him on by free and joyful ways to know and choose the things that are pure and lovely and of good report, make as fair an image as we can find of that loving, patient Wisdom which must be above us all if any good is to come out of our childish race.
—*VI, 38.*

MAY

26. The Cross and the Comforter

The vision of Christ's suffering and death makes it infinitely easier for us to receive the Comforter. It breaks the bonds of that rigid and pedantic notion of God which exhibits him as remote, inflexible, impassible. It shows us that he is great enough and good enough to suffer with us in order to deliver us from sin. It diffuses through the soul the fragrance of a new kind of forgiveness—the only real forgiveness—a forgiveness which not only blots out guilt, but opens the heart's door to the Spirit and restores divine fellowship.
—*XII, 187.*

27. New birth of heaven and earth

How glorious is the vision of that kingdom which Jesus unfolds as he looks forward to the new birth of earth and heaven in the perfect fulfilment of the purpose of God! How absolute is the confidence with which he rests upon God's power to work out all that may be needed to bring about that blessed consummation. The unwavering faith of Jesus in the permanence and worldwide diffusion and ultimate triumph of his kingdom of truth and holiness and love, is not the least—sometimes I think it is the greatest—evidence of his divinity and charm of his gospel.
—*VII, 273.*

MAY

28. Sleeping and waking

To those who trust in the Lord and do good, to those who lie down with thoughts of his mercy and truth, it matters not whether they awake in a curtained chamber or in a wild cavern: "the light is sweet, and it is a pleasant thing to behold the sun."
—*I, 50.*

29. Daily courage

How sweet and clear and steady is the life into which courage enters day by day, not merely in those great flashes of excitement which come in the moments of crisis, but in the presence of the hourly perils, the continual conflict. Not to tremble at the shadows which surround us, not to shrink from the foes who threaten us, not to hesitate and falter and stand despairing still among the perplexities and trials of our life, but to move steadily onward without fear—surely that is what the psalmist meant by good courage and strength of heart, and it is a most comfortable, pleasant, peaceful, and happy virtue.
—*IV, 58.*

MAY

30. Decoration Day

There is considerable talk just now about the New South, as if this were a great discovery which someone had made, or a new region which some fluent orator had created, and as if this discovery or creation would account for the present condition of affairs. But in fact it is just the old South and the old North, anointed with the oil of brotherly love, which has flowed down from the head even to the fringe of the garments.
—I, 241.

31. Voices of hope

Do we hear the voices of hope and cheer rising on every side and answering from land to land, proclaiming the promise of a better day in the future than any that have dawned in the past, acknowledging that when people are like Christ, earth will be like heaven? It is the divinity of King Jesus, manifested in human flesh, real living, and eternal, the hope, the joy, the glory of all creation.
—I, 126.

JUNE

1. A great blessing

It is a great blessing to know God in childhood, so that not a single day need be passed in ignorance of his merciful kindness, not a single trial need be borne without his help, not a single pleasure need be enjoyed as if it were the careless gift of chance or the theft of our own cleverness.
—*I, 22.*

2. Matins

Flowers, when the night is done,
Lift their heads to greet the sun;
Sweetest looks and odors raise,
In a silent hymn of praise.

So my heart would turn away
From the darkness to the day;
Lying open, in God's sight,
As a flower in the light.
—*IX, II.*

JUNE

3. A painting by Murillo

What is this, then, but a formal picture of the Trinity, in which the descending Spirit of all grace is the connecting link between the Father and the Son? Yes, that was the old painter's theology, and it is mine. But when words fail to interpret the mystery of it, and forms and colors do but dimly shadow its meaning, I turn the eyes of my heart towards the Christ-child, who holds fast to the hands of humanity and acknowledges its claim upon him, even while he knows that he came forth from God and the sense of union with his heavenly Father dawns within him. Here is the solution of the secret, not in words, but through a life that, though it is veiled, draws God down to humanity and lifts humanity up towards God.
—III, 226.

4. Contentment

Why should we be disturbed, and harassed, and filled with gloom, at the chances of commerce and the changes of business? Our peace of mind is worth more than all things else, and this we can keep in a log cabin or in a hut of turf. Is not this the lesson which Christ would have us learn from the lilies and the sparrows? God may give us more or less, but so long as we are content, it will always be enough and we cannot want.
—I, 33.

JUNE

5. *Song of a pilgrim soul*

March on, my soul, nor like a laggard stay!
March swiftly on. Yet err not from the way
Where all the nobly wise of old have trod—
The path of faith made by the sons of God.

Follow the marks that they have set beside
The narrow, cloud-swept track, to be
      thy guide:
Follow, and honor what the past has gained,
And forward still, that more may be attained.

Something to learn, and something to forget:
Hold fast the good, and seek the better yet:
Press on, and prove the pilgrim-hope
      of youth—
That Creeds are milestones on the road
      to Truth.
—*IX, 57.*

6. *Be not silent*

Be not ashamed to bow your knees where others can see you. Be not ashamed to sing his praise where others can hear you. There is nothing that can become you so much as to speak well of your heavenly Father.
—*I, 256.*

JUNE

7. Loved into loving

The special, personal, elective love of Christ for his own is not exclusive; it is magnificently and illimitably inclusive. He loved his disciples into loving their fellow human beings. He lifted them into union with God; but he did not lift them out of the world; and every tie that bound them to humanity, every friendship, every fellowship, every link of human intercourse, was to be a channel for the grace of God that brings salvation, that it might appear to all people.
—VII, 310.

8. A cheerful spirit

It is said that a friend once asked the great composer Haydn why his church music was always so full of gladness. He answered, "I cannot make it otherwise. I write according to the thoughts I feel; when I think upon my God my heart is so full of joy that the notes dance and leap from my pen; and since God has given me a cheerful heart, it will be pardoned me that I serve him with a cheerful spirit."

Pardoned? Nay, it will be praised and rewarded. For God looks with approval, and man turns with gratitude, to every one who shows by a cheerful life that faith is a blessing for this world and the next.
—I, 96.

JUNE

9. *The finest roses*

The best rosebush, after all, is not that which has the fewest thorns, but that which bears the finest roses.
—*XIII, 149.*

10. *The river of dreams*

The river of dreams runs silently down
> By a secret way that no man knows;
> But the soul lives on while the
> dream-tide flows

Through the gardens bright, or the
> forests brown;
> And I think sometimes that our whole
> life seems
> To be more than half made up of
> dreams.
> For its changing sights, and its
> passing shows,
> And its morning hopes, and its
> midnight fears,
> Are left behind with the vanished years.

Onward, with ceaseless motion,
The life-stream flows to the ocean—
> And we follow the tide, awake or asleep,
> Till we see the dawn on Love's
> great deep,
> When the bar at the harbor-mouth
> is crossed,
> And the river of dreams in the sea
> is lost.

—*XIV, 83.*

JUNE

11. Art and religion

When Christian theology has fully returned to its vital center in Christ, and its divided forces are reunited—amid the hostile camps and warring elements of modern society—in a simple and potent ministry of deliverance and blessing to all the oppressed and comfortless "in his name"; when art has felt the vivid reality and the ideal beauty of this gospel of the personal entrance of God into the life of humankind, and has come to it for what art needs today more than all else—a deep, living, spiritual impulse and inspiration—then art will render a more perfect service to religion, and religion will give a new elevation to art.
—III, 109.

12. The city and the home

People draw a broad line between the public and the private, and think that the evils of society can be cured without paying any attention to the virtues of the household, or that the purity of family life can be maintained without regard to the atmosphere of society. But the Bible teaches us that the public and the private depend on each other, and that the welfare of the city and the welfare of the home are bound up together.
—I, 225.

JUNE

13. Living prayers

There is no good in praying for anything unless you will also try for it. All the sighs and supplications in the world will not bring wisdom to the heart that fills itself with folly every day, or mercy to the soul that sinks itself in sin, or usefulness and honor to the life that wastes itself in vanity and inanity.
—*I, 21.*

14. The gates of hearing

Through the outer portals of the ear
Only the outer voice of things may pass;
And through the middle doorways of
    the mind
Only the half-formed voice of human
    thoughts,
Uncertain and perplexed with endless doubt;
But through the inmost gate the spirit hears
The voice of that great Spirit who is Life.
Beneath the tones of living things,
    He breathes
A deeper tone than ever ear hath heard;
And underneath the troubled thoughts
    of men,
He thinks forever, and His thought is peace.
Behold, I touch thee once again, my child:
The third and last of those three hidden gates
That closed around thy soul and shut thee in,
Falls open now, and thou shalt truly hear.
—*XIV, 51.*

JUNE

15. Riverside devotions

It is by a river that I would choose to revive old friendships, and to play with the children, and to confess my faults, and to escape from vain, selfish desires, and to cleanse my mind from all false and foolish things that mar the joy and peace of living. Like David's hart, I pant for the water-brooks, and would follow the advice of the philosopher Seneca, who says, "Where a spring rises, or a river flows, there should we build altars."
—*VI, II.*

16. The secret things of God

The Bible does not profess to make people omniscient, but simply to tell them enough to make them good, if they will believe it and live it. It does indeed lift them above the level of their natural ignorance; but even as one who has gained a wider view of the world by ascending a lofty mountain still finds sight circumscribed by a new horizon, so those who receive the revelations which are contained in Holy Scripture still discover a verge beyond which their thought cannot pass, and find themselves shut in by the secret things which belong unto God.
—*IV, 217.*

JUNE

17. Focusing on simplicity

We must get back from the confusions of theology to the simplicity that is in Christ. We must see clearly that our central message is not the gospel of a system, but the gospel of a Person. We must hold fast the true humanity of Jesus in order that we may know what is meant by his true divinity. We must recognize his supreme authority in the interpretation of the Bible itself. We must accept his revelations of human liberty and divine sovereignty. Above all, we must accept his great salvation from the curse of sin.
—*VII, ix.*

18. Pure and undefiled

The world has small need of a religion which consists solely or chiefly of emotions and raptures. But the religion that follows Jesus Christ, alike when he goes up into the high mountain to pray and when he comes down into the dark valley to work; the religion that listens to him, alike when he tells us of the peace and joy of the Father's house and when he calls us to feed his lambs; the religion that is willing to suffer as well as to enjoy, to labor as well as to triumph; the religion that has a soul to worship God, and a heart to love man, and a hand to help in every good cause—is pure and undefiled.
—*IV, 187.*

JUNE

19. Being and becoming

What we do belongs to what we are; and what we are is what becomes of us.
—*VIII, 12.*

20. Being always busy

We have fallen so much into the habit of being always busy that we know not how or when to break it off with firmness. Our business tags after us into the midst of our pleasures, and we are ill at ease beyond the reach of the telegraph and the daily newspaper.
—*XII, 192.*

21. Hidden treasures

Christianity is complete, and has been so ever since it was embodied in the life of Christ. Everyone who has Christ in the heart has the whole of it; nothing can be added, nothing can be taken away. But the understanding of it, the living sense of what it means, comes only by degrees, to different people and to different ages. Even yet, as we gladly believe, the Church has much undiscovered country and many hidden treasures in that territory of truth which she has possessed from the beginning.
—*III, 48.*

JUNE

22. The slender shade of artificial tastes

In the time of adversity one should prepare for prosperity. I fancy there are a good many people unconsciously repeating the mistake of the Canadian farmer—chopping down all the native growths of life, clearing the ground of all the useless pretty things that seem to cumber it, sacrificing everything to utility and success. We fell the last green tree for the sake of raising an extra hill of potatoes, and never stop to think what an ugly, barren place we may have to sit in while we eat them. The ideals, the attachments—yes, even the dreams—of youth are worth saving. For the artificial tastes with which age tries to make good their loss grow very slowly and cast but a slender shade.
—VI, 201.

23. The bravest creature

I suppose a bird is the bravest creature that lives, in spite of its natural timidity. From which we may learn that true courage is not incompatible with nervousness, and that heroism does not mean the absence of fear, but the conquest of it. Who does not remember the first time that they ever ran across a hen partridge with her brood while strolling through the woods in June? How splendidly the old bird forgets herself in her efforts to defend and hide her young!
—XIII, 23.

JUNE

24. *The bulwark of society*

The fear of God is the bulwark of society. Every institution which reinforces it upon the human heart and conscience is of incalculable worth to the community.
—*I, 228.*

25. *This standing place*

God is thy roof to shelter thee. How this truth steadies and confirms the soul! It is like a great rock in the midst of hurrying floods; and from this standing place we can look out serenely upon the mutabilities of life.
—*I, 18.*

26. *The skylark's voice*

The first time that I ever heard the skylark was on the great plain of Salisbury. Sheep were feeding and shepherds were watching nearby. From the contentment of her lowly nest in the grass the songstress rose on quivering wings, pouring out a perfect flood of joy. With infinite courage the feathered atom breasted the spaces of the sky, as if her music lifted her irresistibly upward. With sublime confidence she passed out of sight into the azure; but not out of hearing, for her cheerful voice fell yet more sweetly through the distance, as if it were saying, "Forever, forever!"
—*I, 36.*

27. The Name

The name of Christ was magical; not as a secret and unintelligible incantation, but as the sign of a real person, known and loved. It enlightened and healed and quickened the heart of an age which, like our own, was dark and sorrowful and heavy with doubt. It was the charm which drew people to Christianity out of the abstractions of philosophy and the confusions of idolatry, darkened with a thousand personifications but empty of all true personality. The music of that name rang through all the temple of the church, and to its harmonies her walls were built. The acknowledgment of that name was the mark of Christian discipleship. To confess that "Jesus is the Christ" was the way to enter the church. The symbolism of that name was the mark of Christian worship. The central rites of the church were baptism into Christ and communion with Christ. Fidelity to his name was the crown of Christian martyrdom.
—VII, 64.

JUNE

28. The One who abides

The person of Jesus Christ stands solid in the history of humanity. He is indeed more substantial, more abiding, in human apprehension, than any form of matter, or any mode of force. The conceptions of earth and air and fire and water change and melt around him, as the clouds melt and change around an everlasting mountain peak. All attempts to resolve him into a myth, a legend, an idea—and hundreds of such attempts have been made—have drifted over the enduring reality of his character and left not a trace behind. The result of all criticism, the final verdict of enlightened common sense, is that Christ is historical.
—VII, 58.

29. While we sleep

"God bestows his gifts during the night," says the old German proverb. Sleep itself is a great blessing; and while we sleep the clouds are storing their supplies of moisture, the rivers are performing their ministry of labor on our behalf, the seeds are swelling in the earth, the grain is springing in the fields, the fruits are ripening on the tree, the harvest is growing golden in the mellow darkness of the autumn night; for in truth, if we are wise and diligent, Nature is on our side, and all God's world is busy preparing our bread.
—I, 223.

30. Protecting wings

The only thing that can really darken the soul is something coming between it and God. But that is impossible so long as the soul remembers his presence and love. He touches us on every side with his compassionate care. The troubles and pains of life are all outside of that; they are away beyond the protecting wings, floating by, like little clouds, like hovering hawks; we can wait in security until these "calamities be overpast." Trouble is far off: God is very near. Calamities belong to time: peace is part of eternity.
—I, 47.

JULY

1. *In praise of the tent*

People may say what they will in praise of their houses, and grow eloquent upon the merits of various styles of architecture, but, for our part, we are agreed that there is nothing to be compared with a tent. It is the most venerable and aristocratic form of human habitation. Abraham and Sarah lived in it, and shared its hospitality with angels. It is exempt from the base tyranny of the plumber, the paper hanger, and the carpenter. It is not immovably bound to one dull spot of earth by the chains of a cellar and a system of water pipes. It has a noble freedom of locomotion. It follows the wishes of its inhabitants, and goes with them, a traveling home, as the spirit moves them to explore the wilderness. At their pleasure, new beds of wild flowers surround it, new plantations of trees overshadow it, and new avenues of shining water lead to its ever-open door. What the tent lacks in luxury it makes up in liberty; or rather let us say that liberty itself is the greatest luxury.
—VI, 249.

JULY

2. The journey

But wherever you are, and whoever you may be, there is one thing in which you and I are just alike, at this moment, and in all the moments of our existence. We are not at rest; we are on a journey. Our life is not a mere fact; it is a movement, a tendency, a steady, ceaseless progress towards an unseen goal. We are gaining something, or losing something, every day. Even when our position and our character seem to remain precisely the same, they are changing. For the mere advance of time is a change. It is not the same thing to have a bare field in January and in July. The season makes the difference. The limitations that are childlike in the child are childish in the adult.
—*VIII, II.*

3. Our highest obligation

The inward joy and power of our life, in every sphere, come from the discovery that our highest obligation rests at last upon the law of gratitude. In every tie that binds us we are made free and glad to serve, when we recognize that we have been "bought with a price."
—*IV, 109.*

JULY

4. Independence Day

The love of liberty: there is no deeper passion than this, native to the human heart. To be free, to move in accordance with voluntary choice, to render submission only where it is due, to follow reason and conscience willingly without the compulsion of brute force—this is the instinct of personality. The nobler the race, the more highly developed the individuals, the stronger and more ardent does this passion become. It is no mere self-asserting spirit of revolt against lawful authority, no wild, untrammeled desire to fling the reins upon the neck of appetite and indulge the personal impulses without restraint. The lovers of liberty are always lovers of law. They desire to follow the best, not the worst; and they rebel, not against the restraints of justice, but against the constraints of power; not against the yoke of service, but against the chains of bondage.
—*I, 177.*

JULY

5. The greater kingdom

Let us remember that while these earthly kingdoms are founded upon wealth and power and wisdom, God's kingdom is founded on holiness of character. And though we may achieve greatness in these lower realms, though we may become merchant princes, or political rulers, or kings of thought, the least in the kingdom of heaven, yes, the simplest, poorest child who has known God's love and felt his purifying Spirit in the heart, will be greater than we are, so long as our sole inheritance is in the kingdoms of this world.
—*IV, 160.*

6. The wellspring of abundance

The teaching of Christ differs from that of all other masters in its fontal quality. It is comprised in a little space, but it has an infinite fullness. Its utterance is closely bounded, but its significance is inexaustible.
—*VII, 194.*

JULY

7. The larger hieroglyphs

The psalmists delight in the vision of the world, and their joy quickens their senses to read alike the larger hieroglyphs of glory written in the stars and the delicate tracings of transient beauty on leaf and flower; to hear alike the mighty roaring of the sea and the soft, sweet laughter of the rustling cornfields. But in all these they see and hear the handwriting and the voice of God.
—*XV, 24.*

8. Beyond beauty

It is God's presence that makes the world of the Psalms sublime and beautiful. The direct, piercing, elevating sense of this presence simplifies, enlarges, and ennobles the psalmists' style, and makes it different from other nature poetry. These poets never lose themselves, like Theocritus and Wordsworth and Shelley and Tennyson, in the contemplation and description of natural beauty. They see it, but they always see beyond it.
—*XV, 24.*

JULY

9. Boarders in the world

The people who always live in houses, and sleep on beds, and walk on pavements, and buy their food from butchers and bakers and grocers, are not the most blessed inhabitants of this wide and various earth. The circumstances of their existence are too mathematical and secure for perfect contentment. They live at a second or third hand. They are boarders in the world. Everything is done for them by somebody else.
—XIII, 14.

10. The measure of success

We measure success by accumulation. The measure is false. The true measure is appreciation. The one who loves most has most.
—XIII, 178.

11. The tide of faith

Christianity is something more than a system of doctrines; it is a life, a tone, a spirit, a great current of memories, beliefs, and hopes flowing through millions of hearts. And those who launch their words upon this current find that their words are carried with a strength beyond their own, and freighted often with a meaning which they themselves have not fully understood as it flashed through them.
—II, 274.

JULY

12. Likeness without imitation

Imitation may be the sincerest flattery, but imitation never produces the deepest resemblance. They who imitate are concerned with that which is outward; but kinship of spirit is inward. They who are next of kin to a mastermind will be too great for the work of copyists; they will be influenced, if at all, unconsciously; and though the intellectual relationship may be expressed also in the some external traits of speech and manner, the true likeness will be in the temper of the soul and the sameness of the moral purpose.
—II, 93.

13. A filled vessel

A vessel filled to the brim with water is apt to spill a little when it is shaken. Peter is so full of human nature that, whenever he is excited or agitated, it seems to overflow, and some word or deed comes out, which would be almost childish in its impulsiveness, if it were not for the virile force of the great strong heart behind it. The consequence of this is, that he is more often in trouble, more frequently rebuked and corrected, than any other of the disciples.
—IV, 169.

14. *The tedious life*

Much of the tediousness of highly civilized life comes from its smoothness and regularity.
—XIII, 12

15. *King of the workers*

"Born within a lowly stable, where the cattle
round Me stood,
Trained a carpenter in Nazareth, I have
toiled, and found it good.

"They who tread the path of labor follow
where My feet have trod;
They who work without complaining do the
holy will of God.

"Where the many toil together, there am I
among My own;
Where the tired workman sleepeth, there am
I with him alone."
—XIV, 22.

JULY

16. Whither bound?

We cannot divide our work from ourselves, nor isolate our future from our qualities. A ship might as well try to sail north with her jib, and east with her foresail, and south with her mainsail, as a man to go one way in conduct, and another way in character, and another way in destiny.
—*VIII, 12.*

17. Bearing fruit in old age

In the secluded garden of Christ's College, at Cambridge, there is a mulberry tree which tradition says was planted by John Milton in his student days. I remember sitting on the green turf below it, a few years ago, and looking up at the branches, heavy with age and propped on crutches, and wondering to see that the old tree still brought forth fruit. It was not the size nor the quality of the fruit that impressed me. I hardly thought of that. The strange thing, the beautiful thing, was that, after so many years, the tree was yet bearing.
—*II, 279.*

JULY

18. Two good rules

There are two good rules which ought to be written upon every heart. Never believe anything bad about anybody, unless you positively know that it is true. Never tell even that, unless you feel that it is absolutely necessary, and that God is listening while you tell it.
—I, 49.

19. Talk

Talk is that form of human speech which is exempt from all duties, foreign and domestic. It is the nearest thing in the world to thinking and feeling aloud. It is necessarily not for publication—solely an evidence of good faith and mutual kindness. You tell me what you have seen and what you are thinking about, because you take it for granted that it will interest and entertain me; and you listen to my replies and the recital of my adventures and opinions, because you know I like to tell them, and because you find something in them, of one kind or another, that you care to hear. It is a nice game, with easy, simple rules, and endless possibilities of variation. And if we go into it with the right spirit, and play it for love, without heavy stakes, the chances are that if we happen to be fairly talkable people we shall have one of the best things in the world—a mighty good talk.
—XIII, 59.

JULY

20. *A prayer for light*

Grant us the knowledge that we need
    To solve the questions of the mind;
Light Thou our candle while we read,
    And keep our hearts from going blind.
—IX, 86.

21. *The Fresh Air Fund*

Think of the beautiful charity which carries vast multitudes of little ones every summer out of the crowded city into the fresh air of the country. How did that begin? In the attempt of a country minister to bring a score of poor children to spend a few days in the farmhouses of his scanty parish. What can we do? Nothing. What can God do with us? Anything; whatsoever he will.
—IV, 90.

22. *The point of view*

Indeed, it is not from the highest peaks, according to my experience, that one gets the grandest prospects, but rather from those of middle height, which are so isolated as to give a wide circle of vision, and from which one can see both the valleys and the summits.

It is possible, in this world, to climb too high for pleasure.
—VI, 162.

JULY

23. *The protecting shadow*

"In the shadow of thy wings I take refuge."
How exquisite is the beauty of this figure, and how perfect is the spiritual repose which it expresses! David was not content with an image drawn from the cavern in which he had found shelter. It was not enough for him to say that the care in which he confided was like the great walls and overarching roof of the cave. He felt that God was nearer than these, that he brooded above his people as a mother bird covers her nest with her own feathers. High in the air the cruel hawks go sailing by, but they cannot reach the nest; even their black shadows cannot fall upon it so long as it is protected by the shadow of those other, greater wings.
—I, 46.

24. *Indolence*

Indolence is a virtue. It comes from two Latin words which mean freedom from anxiety or grief. And that is a wholesome state of mind. There are times and seasons when it is even a pious and blessed state of mind. Not to be in a hurry; not to be ambitious or jealous or resentful; not to feel envious of anybody; not to fret about today nor worry about tomorrow—that is the way we ought all to feel at some time in our lives; and that is the kind of indolence in which little rivers faithfully encourage us.
—XIII, 192.

JULY

25. The waking of the soul

And it is well also when the spiritual powers are roused with the physical. It is well when the soul is active and excited; moved and thrilled by feeling, as the flowers in the field are stirred by the morning breeze. Then the sweet odors flow out. The bells do not ring until they swing. The birds do not please us until they leave their nests and begin to warble their sweet notes.
—I, 50.

26. The journey

But wherever you are, and whoever you may be, there is one thing in which you and I are just alike, at this moment, and in all the moments of our existence. We are not at rest; we are on a journey. Our life is not a mere fact; it is a movement, a tendency, a steady, ceaseless progress towards an unseen goal. We are gaining something, or losing something, every day. Even when our position and our character seem to remain precisely the same, they are changing. For the mere advance of time is a change. It is not the same thing to have a bare field in January and in July. The season makes the difference. The limitations that are childlike in the child are childish in the adult.
—VIII, II.

JULY

27. Four fine things

Goodness of heart, freedom of spirit, cheerfulness of temper, and friendliness of disposition—these are four fine things, and doubtless as acceptable to God as they are agreeable to humans. The talkability which springs out of these qualities has its roots in a good soil. On such a plant one need not look for the poison berries of malicious discourse, nor for the Dead Sea apples of frivolous mockery. But fair fruit will be there, pleasant to the sight and good for food, brought forth abundantly according to the season.
—*XIII, 61.*

28. A book for scholar and peasant

Poets like Shakespeare, Milton, and Wordsworth; novelists like Scott and romancers like Hawthorne; essayists like Bacon, Steele, and Addison; critics of life, unsystematic philosophers, like Carlyle and Rushkin—all draw upon the Bible as a treasury of illustrations, and use it as a book equally familiar to themselves and to their readers. It is impossible to put too high a value upon such a universal volume, even as a mere literary possession. It forms a bond of sympathy between the most cultivated and the simplest of the people. The same book lies upon the desk of the scholar and in the cupboard of the peasant.
—*II, 246.*

JULY

29. Adoration

O Thou whose boundless love bestows
    The joy of life, the hope of Heaven;
Thou whose uncharted mercy flows
    O'er all the blessings Thou hast given;
Thou by whose light alone we see;
Thou by whose truth our souls, set free,
Are made imperishably strong;
Hear Thou the solemn music of our song.
—IX, 86.

30. The One who saves

The person of Jesus stands out clear and simple as a powerful Savior of sinful men and women. In his presence, the publican and the harlot felt their hearts dissolve with I know not what unutterable rapture of forgiveness. At his word, the heavy-laden were mysteriously loosed from the imponderable burden of past transgression. He suffered with sinners, and even while he suffered he delivered them from the sharpest of all pains—the pain of conscious and unpardoned evil. He died for sinners, according to his own word; and ever since, his cross has been the sign of rescue for humanity.
—VII, 76.

JULY

31. *Silent fellowship*

That is a chilly and frost-bound disposition which prefers to enjoy its happiness or bear grief alone. The presence of a friend who can feel with us, even though imperfectly; the mere silent presence of a friend, even though he be asleep, as the friends of Jesus were, is something which enhances pleasure and mitigates sorrow in every true and noble heart.
—*IV, 177.*

AUGUST

1. *A clear fountain*

The sacred books of other religions, the commentaries and expositions on the Christian religion, spread before us a vast and intricate expanse, like lakes of truth mixed with error, stretching away into the distance, arm after arm, bay after bay, until we despair of being able even to explore their coasts and trace their windings. When we come back to Christ, we find, not an inland sea of doctrine, but a clear fountain of living water, springing up into everlasting life.
—*VII, 194.*

2. *Giving ourselves to serve*

To behold the vision of God in Christ is to be one of God's elect. But the results of that election depend upon the giving of ourselves to serve the world for Jesus' sake. *Noblesse oblige.*
—*VII, 316.*

AUGUST

3. *A prayer for light*

>Enlarge our vision to behold
>The wonders Thou hast wrought of old;
>Reveal Thyself in every law,
>And gild the towers of truth with holy awe.
>—*IX, 86.*

4. *The unfinished dream*

>Life is an unfinished dream. Even when it is drawn out to its full length, even when an uncommon strength enables us to carry the burden on beyond the limit of threescore and ten, the thread is suddenly cut off, and we fly away in haste. Death is always a surprise. No one is ever quite ready for it. The will is left unwritten. The enterprise halts uncompleted. The good deed is not accomplished. The ones who say, "I will devote my fortune now to the service of God and humanity," fly away suddenly, and their wealth is squandered by the spendthrift heir. The ones who resolve to be reconciled to their enemies and die at peace with all humankind, are cut off in a moment, and the words of repentance and forgiveness are never spoken. It is the old story. Moses, who lived one hundred and twenty years, died too soon, for he never entered the land of his pilgrimage, and his dream was left unfinished.
>—*I, 20.*

5. The life of faith

The ones who take a principle into their hearts commit themselves to an uncertainty; they enter upon an adventure. They must be ready for unexpected calls and new responsibilities. That is the law of the life of faith.
—IV, 140.

6. Critical moments

Every moment of life, I suppose, is more or less of a turning point. Opportunities are swarming around us all the time thicker than gnats at sundown. We walk through a cloud of chances, and if we were always conscious of them they would worry us almost to death.

But happily our sense of uncertainty is soothed and cushioned by habit, so that we can live comfortably with it.
—XIII, 35.

7. Satisfying the reason and the heart

This is what Christ gives us: a view of God in his world which requires faith to accept it, but which, when accepted, satisfies the reason and the heart better than any other view, and becomes the inward source not of doubt and distress, but of certainty and peace.
—VII, 252.

AUGUST

8. Music

Music lends a strange sweetness to the remembrance of the past, and makes the troubles of the present heavier, yet easier to bear. And then it borrows the comfort of hope. It drops the threads of sorrow one by one, and catches the sweet beams of light reflected from the future, and weaves them magically in among its harmonies, blending, brightening, softening the mystic web, until we are enclosed, we know not how, in a garment of consolation, and the cold, tired heart finds itself warmed, and rested, and filled with courage. Most gracious ministry of music! Happy are they who know how to exercise it in simplicity and love; happy they whose life-pilgrimage is cheered and lightened by such service.
—*I, 164.*

9. The liberty of joy

"A man's life consisteth not in the abundance of the things which he possesseth." The land of wealth is not the empire of peace. Joy is not bounded on the north by poverty, on the east by obscurity, on the west by simplicity, and on the south by servitude. It runs far over these borders on every side. The lowliest, plainest, narrowest life may be the sweetest.
—*VII, 289.*

AUGUST

10. Abundant gleaning

What does it profit a person to be the landed proprietor of countless acres unless they can reap the harvest of delight that blooms from every yard of God's earth for the seeing eye and the loving spirit? And who can reap that harvest so closely that there shall not be abundant gleaning left for all mankind? The most that a wide principality can yield to its legal owner is a living. But the real owner can gather from a field of goldenrod, shining in the August sunlight, an unearned increment of delight.
—*XIII, 178.*

11. Infectious kindness

Kindness is contagious. The spirit of harmony trickles down by a thousand secret channels into the inmost recesses of the household life. One truly affectionate soul in a family will exert a sweetening and harmonizing influence upon all its members. It is hard to be angry in the presence of imperturbable good nature. It is well-nigh impossible to be morose in the face of a cheerful and generous helpfulness. Beginning with the highest, the ointment drops even upon those who are unconscious or careless of it, and the whole house is presently filled with its fragrance.
—*I, 241.*

12. Ruling passions

Life is much too large to be expressed in the terms of a single passion. Friendship, patriotism, parental tenderness, filial devotion, the ardor of adventure, the thirst for knowledge, the ecstasy of religion—these all have their dwelling in the heart of man. They mold character. They control conduct. They are stars of destiny shining in the inner firmament. And if art would truly hold the mirror up to nature, it must reflect these greater and lesser lights that rule the day and the night.
—XIII, 100.

13. On the tablets of the heart

Jesus wrote not with a pen upon enduring parchment, nor with a stylus upon imperishable brass: "He stooped / And wrote upon *the unrecording ground*." He would not leave even a single line of manuscript where his followers could preserve it with literal reverence and worship it as a sacred relic. He chose to inscribe his teaching upon no other leaves than those which are folded within the human soul. He chose to trust his words to the faithful keeping of memory and love; and he said of them, with sublime confidence, that they should never pass away. He chose that the truth which he declared and the life which he lived should never be divided, but that they should go down together through the ages.
—VII, 184.

AUGUST

14. The face of the world renewed

But when man abides in tents, after the manner of the early patriarchs, the face of the world is renewed. The vagaries of the clouds become significant. You watch the sky with a lover's look, eager to know whether it will smile or frown. When you lie at night upon your bed of boughs and hear the rain pattering on the canvas close above your head, you wonder whether it is a long storm or only a shower.
—XIII, 15.

15. The dew of Hermon

There is a beautiful legend in the Itinerary of St. Anthony. An old pilgrim narrates that, every morning at sunrise, a handful of dew floated down from Hermon and fell upon the Church of St. Mary, where it was immediately gathered by the Christian physicians, and was found a sovereign remedy for all diseases. What is this dew but the word of Jesus Christ? "This is my commandment, that ye love one another." It falls from heaven upon the church. But it is not meant for her refreshment alone. It is intended to be a cure for the evils of society, spreading from heart to heart, from land to land.
—I, 246.

AUGUST

16. *A wilding strain*

The theory that Adam lived out in the woods for some time before he was put into the garden of Eden "to dress it and to keep it" has an air of probability. How else shall we account for the arboreal instincts that cling to his posterity?

There is a wilding strain in our blood that all the civilization in the world will not eradicate. I never knew a real boy—or, for that matter, a girl worth knowing—who would not rather climb a tree, any day, than walk up a golden stairway.

—*XIII, 84.*

17. *Martin Luther's logic*

Do you remember Martin Luther's reasoning on the subject of "excellent large pike"? He maintains that God would never have created them so good to the taste, if he had not meant them to be eaten. And for the same reason I conclude that this world would never have been left so full of uncertainties, nor human nature framed so as to find a peculiar joy and exhilaration in meeting them, if it had not been divinely intended that most of our amusement and much of our education should come from this source.

—*XIII, 10.*

AUGUST

18. *The daily miracle*

The life of humanity is a demonstrated daily miracle. It shows that the physical laws which we know and the physical forces which we can measure, are traversed by spiritual laws which we do not know and spiritual forces which we cannot measure. It proves the reality and potency of that which is invisible and imponderable.
—XII, 91.

19. *Peculiar pleasure*

There is a peculiar pleasure in catching trout in a place where nobody thinks of looking for them, and at an hour when everybody believes they cannot be caught. It is more fun to take one good fish out of an old, fished-out stream, near at hand to the village, than to fill a basket from some far-famed and well-stocked water. It is the unexpected touch that tickles our sense of pleasure. While life lasts, we are always hoping for it and expecting it. There is no country civilized, no existence so humdrum, that there is not room enough in it somewhere for a lazy, idle brook with hope of happy surprises.
—XIII, 203.

AUGUST

20. *Personal property*

What is property, after all? The law says there are two kinds, real and personal. But it seems to me that the only real property is that which is truly personal, that which we take into our inner life and make our own forever, by understanding and admiration and sympathy and love. This is the only kind of possession that is worth anything.
—*XIII, 176.*

21. *Fortune great or small*

Then come, my friend, forget your foes, and
 leave your fears behind,
And wander forth to try your luck, with
 cheerful, quiet mind;
For be your fortune great or small, you'll
 take what God may give,
And all the day your heart shall say, " 'Tis
 luck enough to live."
—*XIV, 68.*

22. *The purest souls*

The effort after holiness always intensifies the consciousness of sin. The purest souls are those who cling most closely to God as their Redeemer and helper.
—*I, 66.*

AUGUST

23. Under the silent stars

If we can only come back to nature together every year, and consider the flowers and the birds, and confess our faults and mistakes and our unbelief under these silent stars, and hear the river murmuring in return, we shall die young, even though we live long: we shall have a treasure of memories which will be like the twinflower, always a double blossom on a single stem, and carry with us into the unseen world something immortal.
—*VI, 276.*

24. The deeper things

When I talk to you of fisherman's luck, I do not forget that there are deeper things behind it. I remember that what we call our fortunes, good or ill, are but the wise dealing and distributions of a Wisdom higher, and a Kindness greater, than our own. And I suppose that their meaning is that we should learn, by all the uncertainties of our life, even the smallest, how to be brave and steady and temperate and hopeful, whatever comes, because we believe that behind it all there lies a purpose of good, and over it all there watches a Providence of blessing.
—*XIII, 30.*

AUGUST

25. *Faith for a doubting age*

There is a new cry for a Christ who shall fulfil the hopes of all the ages. There is a new love waiting for him, a new devotion ready to follow his call. Doubt, in its nobler aspect—honest, morally earnest doubt—has been a John the Baptist to prepare the way for his coming. The men of today are saying, as certain Greeks said of old, "Sirs, we would see Jesus." The disciple who can lead the questioning souls to him, is the one who has the gospel for an age of doubt.
—*VII, 40.*

26. *The salt of conversation*

The west wind has the good sense to talk about himself occasionally and tell his own experience. The person who will not do that must always be a dull companion. Modest egoism is the salt of conversation: you do not want too much of it; but if it is altogether omitted, everything tastes flat.
—*VI, 133.*

27. *The arrow*

Life is an arrow—therefore you must know
What mark to aim at, how to use the bow—
Then draw it to the head, and let it go!
—*IX, 65.*

AUGUST

28. *The leader as follower*

> "The King will follow Christ, and we the King."

Compare this line with the words of St. Paul: "Be ye followers of me even as I also am of Christ." They teach us that lasting devotion is rendered not to the human, but to the divine. They who would lead others must first learn to follow One who is higher than themselves. Without faith it is not only impossible to please God, but also impossible to rule people.
—*II, 253.*

29. *Verve*

In talk it is not correctness of grammar nor elegance of enunciation that charms us; it is spirit, *verve*, the sudden turn of humor, the keen pungent taste of life. For this reason a touch of dialect, a flavor of brogue, is delightful. Any dialect is classic that has conveyed beautiful thoughts. Who that ever talked with the poet Tennyson, when he let himself go, over the pipes, would miss the savor of his broad-rolling Lincolnshire vowels, now heightening the humor, now deepening the pathos, of his genuine speech?
—*XIII, 67.*

AUGUST

30. Restful talks

Every afternoon there were long walks with the Mistress in the old-fashioned garden, where wonderful roses were blooming; or through the dark, fir-shaded den where the wild brook dropped down to join the river; or out upon the high moor under the waning orange sunset. Every night there were luminous and restful talks beside the open fire in the library, when the words came clear and calm from the heart, unperturbed by the vain desire of saying brilliant things, which turns so much of our conversation into a combat of wits instead of an interchange of thoughts. Talk like this is possible only between two. The arrival of a third person sets the lists for a tournament, and offers the prize of approbation for a verbal victory. But where there are only two, the armor is laid aside, and there is no call to thrust and parry.
—*VI, 108.*

AUGUST

31. Fame

Well, then, what shall we say of fame? Here again, we must be careful to discriminate between the thing itself and other things which are often confused with it. Fame is simply what our fellow human beings think and say of us. It may be worldwide; it may only reach to a single country or city; it may be confined to a narrow circle of society. Translated in one way, fame is glory; translated in another way, it is merely notoriety. It is a thing which exists, of course; for the thoughts of other people about us are just as actual as our thoughts about ourselves, or as the character and conduct with which those thoughts are concerned. But the three things do not always correspond.
—*VIII, 23.*

SEPTEMBER

1. *The fire on the altar*

Religion without a great hope would be like an altar without a living fire.
—*V, 13.*

2. *High ownership*

How foolishly we train ourselves for the work of life! We give our most arduous and eager efforts to the cultivation of those faculties which will serve us in the competitions of the forum and the marketplace. But if we were wise, we should care infinitely more for the unfolding of those inward, secret, spiritual powers by which alone we can become the owners of anything that is worth having. Surely God is the great proprietor. Yet all his works he has given away. He holds no titles or deeds. The one thing that is his, is the perfect understanding, the perfect joy, the perfect love, of all things that he has made. To a share in this high ownership he welcomes all who are poor in spirit. This is the earth which the meek inherit. This is the heritage of the saints in light.
—*XIII, 179.*

SEPTEMBER

3. *Faithful work*

There the workman saw his labor taking
   form and bearing fruit,
Like a tree with splendid branches rising
   from a humble root.

Looking at the distant city, temples, houses,
   domes, and towers,
Felix cried in exultation: "All the mighty
   work is ours.

"Every mason in the quarry, every builder on
   the shore,
Every chopper in the palm grove, every
   raftman at the oar—

"Hewing wood and drawing water, splitting
   stones and cleaving sod—
All the dusty ranks of labor, in the regiment
   of God,

"March together toward His triumph, do the
   task His hands prepare:
Honest toil is holy service: faithful work is
   praise and prayer."
—*XIV, 17.*

SEPTEMBER

4. The lasting ideal

The one ideal that is pure and permanent and satisfying, the one ideal that actually has had power to keep itself alive and prove itself victorious over the disintegrating forces of sin and death, is the ideal of Jesus Christ. The men and women who have built upon that foundation have left behind them the most enduring and glorious work, even in the very domain where the human ideals have been erected as supreme.
—IV, 250.

5. Late blossoms

There is a breath of fragrance on the cool shady air beside our little stream, that seems familiar. It is the first week of September. Can it be that the twinflower of June, the delicate *Linnaea borealis*, is blooming again? Yes, here is the threadlike stem lifting its two frail pink bells above the bed of shining leaves. How dear an early flower seems when it comes back again and unfolds its beauty in a St. Martin's summer! How delicate and suggestive is the faint, magical odor! It is like a renewal of the dreams of youth.
—VI, 276.

6. The variable order

A settled, unchangeable, clearly foreseeable order of things does not suit our constitution. It tends to melancholy and a fatty heart. Creatures of habit we are undoubtedly; but it is one of our most fixed habits to be fond of variety. The man who is never surprised does not know the taste of happiness, and unless the unexpected sometimes happens to us, we are most grievously disappointed.
—XIII, 12.

7. The land of gold

There are multitudes of people in the world today who are steering and sailing for Ophir, simply because it is the land of gold. What will they do if they reach their desired haven? They do not know. They do not even ask the question. They will be rich. They will sit down on their gold.

Let us look our desires squarely in the face! To win riches, to have a certain balance in the bank, and a certain rating on the exchange, is a real object, a definite object; but it is a frightfully small object for the devotion of a human life, and a bitterly disappointing reward for the loss of an immortal soul. If wealth is our desired haven, we may be sure that it will not satisfy us when we reach it.
—VIII, 23.

SEPTEMBER

8. Rising after rest

A good night makes a good morning. When the eyes have closed with pure and peaceful thoughts, they are refreshed with the sleep which God giveth to his beloved, and they open with cheerful confidence and grateful pleasure.
—I, 50.

9. The sabbath of the fields

It was the benediction hour. The placid air of the day shed a new tranquility over the consoling landscape. The heart of the earth seemed to taste a repose more perfect than that of common days. A hermit thrush, far up the vale, sang his vesper hymn; while the swallows, seeking their evening meal, circled above the river-fields without an effort, twittering softly, now and then, as if they must give thanks. Slight and indefinable touches in the scene, perhaps the mere absence of the tiny human figures passing along the road or laboring in the distant meadows, perhaps the blue curls of smoke rising lazily from the farmhouse chimneys, or the family groups sitting under the maple trees before the door, diffused a sabbath atmosphere over the world.
—XIII, 174.

SEPTEMBER

10. Trust

"Every man is immortal until his work is done." So long as God has anything for us to do in the world he will take care of us and deliver us from danger. We may lay aside all anxiety and fear. We may rejoice in the stream of inward peace which makes gold the city of God. We may go forth to our labors and our conflicts with good courage and a cheerful heart. Be sure that nothing can harm you while you are with him.
—*I, 142.*

11. Nature's generosity

All through the summer that is past, the sun has been shining and the rain has been falling on the fields without regard to the moral or religious differences of their owners. There is no peculiar blessing on Protestant potatoes. The corn and pumpkins in the stingy farmer's fields are ripening just as surely and just as abundantly as those which have been planted and hoed by the most generous of men. All you have to do is to sow the seed and till the soil, and Nature will do the rest without asking what manner of man you are.
—*IV, 193.*

SEPTEMBER

12. *The precious ointment*

Let us never be so foolish as to think that it makes no difference whether we believe or not. Faith is the soul of conduct; faith is the bloom, the breath, the vital power of religion; without it, virtue is the alabaster box, empty; faith is the precious ointment whose fragrance fills the house. Therefore without faith it is impossible to please God.
—IV, 47.

13. *The sadness of youth*

There is a sadness of youth into which the old cannot enter. It seems to them unreal and causeless. But it is even more bitter and burdensome than the sadness of age. There is a sting of resentment in it, a fever of angry surprise that the world should so soon be a disappointment, and life so early take on the look of a failure. It has little reason in it, perhaps, but it has all the more weariness and gloom, because the one who is oppressed by it feels dimly that it is an unnatural and an unreasonable thing, that they should be separated from the joy of their companions, and tired of living before they have fairly begun to live.
—XI, 4.

SEPTEMBER

14. *The heart*

The heart, which can win such victory out of its darkest defeat and reap such harvest from the furrows of the grave, is neither sprung from dust nor destined to return to it.
—II, 150.

15. *True to the light*

"What had he to fear? What had he to live for? He had given away the last remnant of his tribute for the King. He had parted with the last hope of finding him. The quest was over, and it had failed. But, even in that thought, accepted and embraced, there was peace. It was not resignation. It was not submission. It was something more profound and searching. He knew that all was well, because he had done the best that he could, from day to day. He had been true to the light that had been given to him. He had looked for more. And if he had not found it, if a failure was all that came out of his life, doubtless that was the best that was possible. He had not seen the revelation of "life everlasting, incorruptible and immortal." But he knew that even if he could live his earthly life over again, it could not be otherwise than it had been."
—V, 67.

SEPTEMBER

16. The glory of life

The glory of our life below
Comes not from what we do, or what
>we know,
But dwells forevermore in what we are.
There is an architecture grander far
Than all the fortresses of war,
More inextinguishably bright
Than learning's lonely towers of light.
Framing its walls of faith and hope and love
In deathless souls of men, it lifts above
The frailty of our earthly home
>An everlasting dome;
The sanctuary of the human host,
The living temple of the Holy Ghost.
—*IX, 84.*

17. The thought of God

The thought of the divine excellence and beauty, how far it is exalted above us and yet how sweetly it shines upon us; how it belongs to the lofty and eternal sphere of heaven, but also to the lowly and familiar sphere of earth; how it rises like the sun, far away from us, and yet sheds its light and joy upon us and upon every living thing—this is the most sublime, comforting, and elevating thought that can ever visit the soul.
—*I, 51.*

SEPTEMBER

18. *The greatest gift*

The vision of God in Christ is the greatest gift in the world. It binds those who receive it to the highest and most consecrated life.
—*VII, 316.*

19. *A wide aim*

To desire and strive to be of some service to the world, to aim at doing something which shall really increase the happiness and welfare and virtue of mankind—this is a choice which is possible for all of us; and surely it is a good haven to sail for.

The more we think of it, the more attractive and desirable it becomes. To do some work that is needed, and to do it thoroughly well; to make our toil count for something in adding to the sum total of what is actually profitable for humanity; to make two blades of grass grow where one grew before, or, better still, to make one wholesome idea take root in a mind that was bare and fallow; to make our example count for something on the side of honesty, and cheerfulness, and courage, and good faith, and love—this is an aim for life which is very wide, as wide as the world, and yet very definite, as clear as light.
—*VIII, 26.*

SEPTEMBER

20. Poetry

The true mission of poetry is to increase joy. It must, indeed, be sensitive to sorrow and acquainted with grief. But it has wings given to it in order that it may bear us up into the ether of gladness.

There is no perfect joy without love. Therefore love poetry is the best. But the highest of all love poetry is that which celebrates, with the Psalms, "that Love which is and was / My Father and my Brother and my God."
—*XV, 26.*

21. Faith and freedom

Religion is life, and it must grow under the laws of life. Faith is simply the assertion of spiritual freedom; it is the first adventure of the soul. Make that adventure towards God, make that adventure towards Christ, and the soul will know that it is alive. So it enters upon that upward course which leads through the liberty of the children of God to the height of heaven, "Where love is an unerring light / And joy its own security."
—*VII, 242.*

SEPTEMBER

22. Rich and poor

I do not mean to say that the possession of much money is always a barrier to real wealth of mind and heart. Nor would I maintain that all the poor of this world are rich in faith and heirs of the kingdom. But some of them are. And if some of the rich of this world (through the grace of God with whom all things are possible) are also modest in their tastes, and gentle in their hearts, and open in their minds, and ready to be pleased with unbought pleasures, they simply share in the best things which are provided for all.
—*XIII, 177.*

23. Evidences

An honest, earnest, true heart; a hand that will not stain itself with unjust gain, or hold an unequal balance, or sign a deceitful letter, or draw an unfair contract; a tongue that will not twist itself to a falsehood or take up an evil report; a soul that points as true as a compass to the highest ideal of manhood or womanhood—these are the marks and qualities of God's people everywhere.
—*I, 66.*

SEPTEMBER

24. The Bible as literature

As the worshippers in the Temple would observe the art and structure of the carven beams of cedar and the lily work on the tops of the pillars the more attentively because they beautified the house of their God, so the one who has religious faith in the Bible will study more eagerly and carefully the literary forms of the book in which the Holy Spirit speaks forever.
—*XV, 6.*

25. Talkative and talkable

A talkative person is like an English sparrow—a bird that cannot sing, and will sing, and ought to be persuaded not to try to sing. But a talkable person has the gift that belongs to the wood thrush and the veery and the wren, the oriole and the white-throat and the rose-breasted grosbeak, the mocking bird and the robin (sometimes); and the brown thrush; yes, the brown thrush has it to perfection, if you can catch them alone—the gift of being interesting, charming, delightful, in the most offhand and various modes of utterance.
—*XIII, 57.*

SEPTEMBER

26. Learn to endure

They who know only how to enjoy, and not to endure, are ill-fitted to go down the stream of life through such a world as this.
—*XIII, 29.*

27. Small packages

Size is not the measure of excellence. Perfection lies in quality, not in quantity. Concentration enhances pleasure, gives it a point, so that it goes deeper.
—*XIII, 81.*

28. Differing views

It is not necessary that everybody should take the same view of life that pleases us. The world would not get on very well without people who preferred parlor cars to canoes, and patent leather shoes to India rubber boots, and ten-course dinners to picnics in the woods.

But why should we neglect our opportunities for simplicity? The nervous disease of civilization might prevail all around us, but that ought not to destroy our grateful enjoyment of the lucid intervals that are granted to us by a merciful Providence.
—*XIII, 190.*

SEPTEMBER

29. *A new inspiration*

All around the circle of human doubt and despair, where men and women are going out to enlighten and uplift and comfort and strengthen their fellow human beings under the perplexities and burdens of life, we hear the cry for a gospel which shall be divine, and therefore sovereign and unquestionable and sure and victorious. All through the noblest aspirations and efforts and hopes of our age of doubt, we feel the longing, and we hear the demand, for a new inspiration of Christian faith.
—VII, 39.

30. *The coming day*

The day is coming when all shadows shall depart and light be everywhere. The day is coming when all rebellion shall cease and peace be everywhere. The day is coming when all sorrow shall vanish and joy be everywhere. The day is coming when all discord shall be silent, and angels leaning from the battlements of heaven shall hear but one word encircling earth with music: "All nations shall call him BLESSED."
—I, 126.

OCTOBER

1. The reservoir

The sense of absolute confidence in Christ as the perfect example of goodness, and of thorough loyalty to him as the Master of noble life, is the hidden reservoir of moral force. The charities of Christendom are the distributing system. Not more instant and more complete would be the dryness on Manhattan Island if the great dam among the Croton hills were broken and all the lakes and streams dried up, than the drought that would fall upon the beneficence of the world if there were a sudden break in the reservoir of love and loyalty in Christian hearts to their moral Master, or a stoppage of the myriad and multiform feeders which keep it full by preaching Christ.
—*VII, 171.*

OCTOBER

2. *"The pure in heart"*

There are few who have not felt the lofty attraction of the teachings of Christ, in which the ideal of holiness shines so far above our reach, while we are continually impelled to climb towards it. Especially these very words about perfection, which he spoke in the Sermon on the Mount, have often lifted us upward just because they point our aspirations to a goal so high that it seems inaccessible.
—II, 249.

3. *The water of life*

To come into vital contact with God, not as a remote thought, but as a living Person; to feel that he who made the universe is not only the Eternal Wisdom but the wise God, not only the Infinite Love but the loving Father; to be assured by touch of soul that he is an ever-present reality, and to perceive the gentle flow of his affection within the channel of the heart—this is the water of everlasting life, the only draught that can truly quench the craving of the spirit.
—I, 165.

OCTOBER

4. Fellowship

The Psalms breathe a spirit of human fellowship even when they are most intensely personal. The poet rejoices or mourns in solitude, it may be, but not alone. He is one of the people. He is conscious always of the ties that bind him to his fellow human beings.
—XV, 16.

5. The great elegy

Many beautiful poems, and some so noble that they are forever illustrious, have blossomed in the valley of the shadow of death. But among them all none is more rich in significance, more perfect in beauty of form and spirit, or more luminous with the triumph of light and love over darkness and mortality, than Tennyson's *In Memoriam*, the greatest of English elegies.
—II, 131.

OCTOBER

6. October 6, 1892, Tennyson's death

From the misty shores of midnight, touched
    with splendors of the moon,
To the singing tides of heaven, and the light
    more clear than noon,
Passed a soul that grew to music till it was
    with God in tune.

Brother of the greatest poets, true to nature,
    true to art;
Lover of Immortal Love, uplifter of the
    human heart;
Who shall cheer us with high music, who
    shall sing, if thou depart?

Silence here—for love is silent, gazing on the
    lessening sail;
Silence here—for grief is voiceless when the
    mighty poets fail;
Silence here—but far beyond us, many
    voices crying, Hail!
   —*IX, 35.*

7. *In memoriam*

The record of a faith sublime,
> And hope, through clouds, far-off
>> discerned;
> The incense of a love that burned
Through pain and doubt defying Time:

A light that gleamed across the wave
> Of darkness, down the rolling years,
> Piercing the heavy mist of tears—
A rainbow shining o'er the grave:

The story of a soul at strife
> That learned at last to kiss the rod,
> And passed through sorrow up to God,
From living to a higher life.
—*IX, 46.*

OCTOBER

8. A poet for the times

If this age of ours, with its renaissance of art and its catholic admiration of the beautiful in all forms, classical and romantic; with its love of science and its joy in mastering the secrets of Nature; with its deep passion of humanity protesting against social wrongs and dreaming of social regeneration; with its introspective spirit searching the springs of character and action; with its profound interest in the problems of the unseen, and its reaction from the theology of the head to the religion of the heart—if this age of ours is a great age, then Tennyson is a great poet, for he is the clearest, sweetest, strongest voice of the century.
—II, 343.

9. Love—a working force

The various kinds of energy which are developed from the heart are not more real, nor more powerful, than the actual working force which is developed in the world from love in the inner life of man.
—XII, 91.

OCTOBER

10. Changes of duty

The Samaritan who rode down from Jerusalem to Jericho had nothing to do in the morning but follow that highway, and take care that his beast did not stumble or hurt itself, or get tired out so that it could not finish the journey. He was just a solitary horseman, and all that he needed to do was to have a good seat in the saddle and a light hand on the bit. But at noon, when he came to the place where that unknown pilgrim lay senseless and bleeding beside the road—then, in a moment, the Samaritan's duty changed, and God called him to be a rescuer, a nurse, a helper of the wounded.
—*IV, 140.*

11. Home thoughts in a far country

Sin is the separation of man from God. The *sense* of sin is God's unbroken hold upon the heart of humanity.

The sacrifices on myriad altars bear witness to it. The prayers of penitence rising from all dark corners of the earth bear witness to it. The tremulous homeward turnings of innumerable souls from far countries of misery and loneliness bear witness to it.

"Father, I have sinned against heaven and in thy sight, and am no more worthy to be called thy son!" But mark—he still says, *Father!*
—*XII, 48.*

12. *Not one forgotten*

We do not dare to think that there is even one forgotten, despised, disowned. God will not let us think so. With clear, sweet, but silent voice, he is assuring every human child that the heavens above their heads are not empty, but filled with the presence of a divine Father, and that the earth beneath their feet is not a strange and desert place, but the soil of home, in which paternal bounty will make provision for wants. Every ray of sunlight that falls from heaven, every drop of rain that waters the fruitful ground, is saying to the heart of humanity, "My child, this a Father's impartial kindness sends to thee."
—*IV, 200.*

13. *Personal religion*

This is the true meaning of personal religion: not merely that the faith and love and hope of the believer proceed from a personal source within themselves and are independent of all outward circumstances, but that they center in a personal Being, who has made us for himself and bestows himself upon us. And this truth finds its most perfect disclosure in the incarnation of Jesus Christ.
—*I, 105.*

14. Proof and bond

For the spiritual as truly as for the temporal life the rule is, "Nothing venture, nothing win." And is it not infinitely nobler and more inspiring to enter upon a career which is to run so close to God that he can speak into it and fill it with new meanings, new possibilities, new tasks, at any moment—is not that infinitely finer and more glorious than to make a contract to do a certain thing for a certain price, as if God were a manufacturer and we were his mill-hands? It seems to me that this is the very proof and bond of friendship with him, this calling of faith to an unlimited and undefined obedience.
—*IV, 142.*

15. A living tie

When you can talk to God, when you can really tell him what is in your heart, then you have found religion. For religion is nothing else than a living tie, a channel of vital intercourse between God and man.
—*I, 169.*

OCTOBER

16. *The assurance of love*

If the father has his inclinations towards his children, so also have the children their inclinations towards their father. It is not enough for them to dwell in his house, sheltered beneath his roof and fed at his table. They crave his affection; the words of his forgiveness when they have done wrong; the words of his approval when they have done right; the assurance of his fatherly love. And so our hearts naturally desire the assurance of the love of God. Where else can we find it save in Jesus Christ? When he speaks to us, we know that our heavenly Father careth for us with a tenderness which he does not give to any but his children. When he dies for us, we know that God, who spared not his own Son, but freely delivered him up for us all, shall also with him freely give us all things. When he rises again for us, we know that death is conquered, and that there is a mansion for us in the Father's heavenly house.
—I, 258.

17. *Climbing upward*

The doctrine of the forgiveness of sins and good hope through grace is the most precious to those who are climbing upward, with painful steps, to seek the face of God.
—I, 66.

OCTOBER

18. *A pleasant pilgrimage*

The wild desire to be forever racing against old Father Time is one of the killjoys of modern life. That ancient traveler is sure to beat you in the long run, and as long as you are trying to rival him, he will make your life a burden. But if you will only acknowledge his superiority and profess that you do not approve of racing after all, he will settle down quietly beside you and jog along like the most companionable of creatures. It is a pleasant pilgrimage in which the journey itself is part of the destination.
—VI, 125.

19. *Daily sacrifice*

God does not show us exactly what it will cost to obey him. He asks us only to give what he calls for from day to day. Here is one sacrifice right in front of us that we must make now in order to serve God—some evil habit to be given up, some lust of the flesh to be crucified and slain—and that is our trial for today.
—IV, 136.

OCTOBER

20. *The warm pulse of humanity*

We must feel the warm pulse of humanity in the Psalms in order to comprehend their meaning and eternal worth. So far as we can connect them with the actual experience of the human race, this will help us to appreciate their reality and power.
—*XV, 15.*

21. *The fortress*

Be Thou our strength when war's wild gust
    Rages around us, loud and fierce;
Confirm our souls and let our trust
    Be like a wall that none can pierce;
Give us the courage that prevails,
The steady faith that never fails,
Help us to stand in every fight
Firm as a fortress to defend the right.
—*IX, 86.*

22. *Gladness and luck*

When you have good luck in anything, you ought to be glad. Indeed, if you are not glad, you are not really lucky.
—*XIII, 27.*

OCTOBER

23. *A renaissance*

With the materialism, the sensuality, the pride of our age, Christianity stands in conflict. With the altruism, the humanity, the sympathy of our age, Christianity must stand in loving and wise alliance. A simpler creed and a nobler life will prepare the way for a renaissance of religion greater and more potent than the world has known for centuries. It seems as if we stood on the brightening border of the new day. The watchword of its coming is the personal gospel of Jesus Christ, in whom we find the ideal man and the real God.
—*VII, xi.*

24. *Life and love*

"What means the voice of Life?" She
    answered, "Love!
For love is life, and they who do not love
Are not alive. But every soul that loves,
Lives in the heart of God and hears
    Him speak."
—*XIV, 53.*

OCTOBER

25. Little memories

You have half forgotten many a famous scene that you traveled far to look upon. You cannot clearly recall the sublime peak of Mont Blanc, the roaring curve of Niagara, the vast dome of St. Peter's. The music of Patti's crystalline voice has left no distinct echo in your remembrance, and the blossoming of the century plant is dimmer than the shadow of a dream. But there is a nameless valley among the hills where you can still trace every curve of the stream, and see the foam-bells floating on the pool below the bridge, and the long moss wavering in the current. There is a rustic song of a girl passing through the fields at sunset, that still repeats its far-off cadence in your listening ears. There is a small flower trembling on its stem in some hidden nook beneath the open sky, that never withers through all the changing years; the wind passeth over it, but it is not gone—it abides forever in your soul, an unfading word of beauty and truth.
—VI, 105.

OCTOBER

26. The Keyword

John turned to him, and his tone softened as he said, "My son, you have sinned deeper than you know. The word with which you parted so lightly is the keyword of all life and joy and peace. Without it the world has no meaning, and existence no rest, and death no refuge. It is the word that purifies love, and comforts grief, and keeps hope alive forever. It is the most precious thing that ever ear has heard, or mind has known, or heart has conceived. It is the name of him who has given us life and breath and all things richly to enjoy; the name of him who, though we may forget him, never forgets us; the name of him who pities us as you pity your suffering child; the name of him who, though we wander far from him, seeks us in the wilderness, and sent his son, even as his son has sent me this night, to breathe again that forgotten name in the heart that is perishing without it. Listen, my son, listen with all your soul to the blessed name of God our Father."

—*XI, 69.*

OCTOBER

27. Joy and peace

That Christ's mission was one of joy and peace needs no proof. The New Testament is a book that throbs and glows with inexpressible gladness. It is the one bright spot in the literature of the first century. The Christians were the happiest people in the world. Poor, they were rich; persecuted, they were exultant; martyred, they were victorious. The secret of Jesus, as they knew it, was a blessed secret. It filled them with the joy of living. Their watchword was, "Rejoice and be exceeding glad."
—XII, 101.

28. Remember

Remember that in this world every mountaintop of privilege is girdled by the vales of lowly duty.

Remember that the transfiguration of the soul is but the preparation and encouragement for the sacrifice of the life.

Remember that we are not to tarry in the transitory radiance of Mount Hermon, but to press on to the enduring glory of Mount Zion, and that we can only arrive at that final and blessed resting place by the way of Mount Calvary.
—IV, 189.

OCTOBER

29. Everyday courage

Courage in the broader sense is an everyday virtue. It includes the possibility of daring, if it be called for; but from hour to hour, in the long, steady run of life, courage manifests itself in quieter, humbler forms—in patience under the little trials, in perseverance in distasteful labors, in endurance of suffering, in resistance of continual and familiar temptations, in hope and cheerfulness and kindness, and such sweet, homely virtues as may find a place in the narrowest and most uneventful life.
—*IV, 63.*

30. The boat and the current

The Christian who says, "I know the power of God, and I am trusting in that to save me, and sustain me, and make me useful, and bring me to heaven," and yet makes no real effort to be good or to do good, is like a man sitting on the bank of a mighty river, and casting chips upon its sweeping tide, and saying, "This river is able to bear me to my journey's end." What you need to do is to push your boat out into the current, and feel its resistless force, and move onward with it. Then you will experience the power that now you only know about.
—*IV, 95.*

OCTOBER

31. En voyage

Are you richer today than you were yesterday? No? Then you are a little poorer. Are you better today than you were yesterday? No? Then you are a little worse. Are you nearer to your port today than you were yesterday? Yes—you must be a little nearer to some port or other; for since your ship was first launched upon the sea of life, you have never been still for a single moment; the sea is too deep, you could not find an anchorage if you would; there can be no pause until you come into port.
—*VIII, II.*

NOVEMBER

1. Not wide, but deep

The things that are revealed belong unto us and to our children forever—is not that what our hearts desire and crave? A religion which shall really belong to us, be a part of us, enter into us, abide with us, and not with us only, but with our children, forever. Not many doctrines, but solid. It need not be very wide, but it must be very deep. It must go down to the bottom of our hearts and dwell there as a living certainty.
—*IV, 231.*

2. The desired haven

If your choice is right, and if your desire is real, so that you will steer and strive with God's help to reach the goal, you shall never be wrecked or lost.

For of every soul that seeks to arrive at usefulness, which is the service of Christ, and at holiness, which is the likeness of Christ, and at heaven, which is the eternal presence of Christ, it is written: "So he bringeth them unto their desired haven."
—*VIII, 37.*

NOVEMBER

3. *A November daisy*

Once the daisies gold and white
Sea-like through the meadows rolled:
Once my heart could hardly hold
All its pleasures—I remember,
In the flood of youth's delight
Separate joys were lost to sight.
That was summer! Now November
Sets the perfect flower apart;
Gives each blossom of the heart
Meaning, beauty, grace unknown—
Blooming late and all alone.
—XIV, 76.

4. *Inspiration and gratitude*

The inspiration of the service that we render in this world to our homes, our country, our fellow human beings, springs from the recognition that a price has been paid for us; the vital power of noble conduct rises from the deep fountain of gratitude, which flows not with water, but with warm heart's blood. How then shall a like power come into our religion, how shall it be as real, as living, as intimate, as our dearest human tie, unless we know and feel that God has paid a price for us, that he has bought us with his own precious life?
—IV, 116.

NOVEMBER

5. Self-revelations of the heart

The Psalms are rightly called lyrics because they are chiefly concerned with the immediate and imaginative expression of real feeling. It is the personal and emotional note that predominates. They are inward, confessional, intense; outpourings of the quickened spirit; self-revelations of the heart. It is for this reason that we should never separate them in our thought from the actual human life out of which they sprang.
—XV, 15.

6. Higher and holier

"Public office is a public trust." The discharge of duty to one's fellow human beings, the work of resisting violence and maintaining order and righting the wrongs of the oppressed, is higher and holier than the following of visions. The service of mankind is the best worship of God.
—II, 178.

NOVEMBER

7. Gifts of nature

The results of education and social discipline in humanity are fine. It is a good thing that we can count upon them. But at the same time let us rejoice in the play of native traits and individual vagaries. Cultivated manners are admirable, yet there is a sudden touch of inborn grace and courtesy that goes beyond them all. No array of accomplishments can rival the charm of an unsuspected gift of nature, brought suddenly to light. I once heard a peasant girl singing down the Austrian Traunthal, and the echo of her song outlives, in the hearing of my heart, all memories of the grand opera.
—XIII, 88.

8. The form of the heart's hope

As a man thinketh in his heart, so is he, and so is his world. For those whose thoughts are earthly and sensual, this is a beast's world. For those whose thoughts are high and noble and heroic, it is a hero's world. The strength of wishes transforms the very stuff of our existence, and molds it to the form of our heart's inmost desire and hope.
—VIII, 35.

9. The human life of God

The Christ of the Gospels is bone of our bone, flesh of our flesh, mind of our mind, heart of our heart. He is in subjection to his parents as a child. He grows to manhood. His character is unfolded by discipline. He labors for daily bread, and prays for divine grace. He hungers, and thirsts, and sleeps, and rejoices, and weeps. He is anointed with the Spirit for his ministry. He is tempted. He is lonely and disappointed. He asks for information. He confesses ignorance. He interprets the facts of nature and life with a prophetic insight.
—VII, 144.

10. The divine mystery

Anything that a telescope could discover among the stars, anything that logic could define and explain and fit into an exact philosophical system, would not be God. For it belongs to his very essence that he transcends our thought, and that his judgments are unsearchable and his ways past finding out. We do not know anything about God unless we know that we cannot know him perfectly.
—IV, 216.

NOVEMBER

11. *The joy of living*

Jesus does not differ from other masters in that he teaches us to scorn earthly joy. The divine difference is that he teaches us how to attain earthly joy, under all circumstances, in prosperity and in adversity, in sickness and in health, in solitude and in society, by taking his yoke upon us, and doing the will of God, and so finding rest unto our souls. That is the debt which every child of God owes not only to God, but also to their own soul—to find the real joy of living.
—*VII, 293.*

12. *Love*

The truth is that love, considered merely as the preference of one person for another of the opposite sex, is not "the greatest thing in the world." It becomes great only when it leads on, as it often does, to heroism and self-sacrifice and fidelity. Its chief value for the interpreter of art lies not in itself, but in its quickening relation to the other elements of life. It must be seen and shown in its due proportion, and in harmony with the broader landscape.
—*XIII, 102.*

NOVEMBER

13. *The late-blooming flower*

Nay, I wrong you, little flower,
Reading mournful mood of mine
In your looks, that give no sign
Of a spirit dark and cheerless:
You possess the heavenly power
That rejoices in the hour,
Glad, contented, free, and fearless—
Lifts a sunny face to heaven
When a sunny day is given;
Makes a summer of its own,
Blooming late and all alone.
—*XIV, 75.*

14. *Art and faith*

Men have assured us, in these latter days, that faith and art have parted company; that faith is dead, and art must live for itself alone. But while they were saying these things in melancholy essays and trivial verses, which denied a spiritual immortality and had small prospect of a literary one, the two highest artists of the century, Tennyson and Browning, were setting their music to the keynote of an endless life, and prophesying with the harp, according as it is written: "I believe, and therefore sing."
—*II, 301.*

NOVEMBER

15. An applied creed

God has revealed himself in Christ in order that we may love him and live with him and be like him. If we will do this we shall be sure of him, and help other men to be sure of him too. The best evidences of religion are holy and kind and useful and godly lives, really molded and controlled by the divine Christ. A short creed well believed and honestly applied is what we need.
—IV, 232.

16. Living faith

When a Christian means one whose word is his bond, who can be trusted with untold treasure without fear of his stealing, whose praise is an honor and whose friendship is a jewel of priceless value; one who does his duty towards his fellow human beings as a service to his God; one whom you can more certainly trust to paint your house, or make your clothes, or draw your will, or take care of the health of your family, because that person is a Christian; one whose outward integrity is the proof of inward purity—then the church will have great praise and large triumph.
—I, 66.

NOVEMBER

17. *Reunion*

To my mind the most beautiful of all the references to the New Testament is the passage in Tennyson's *In Memoriam* which describes the reunion of Mary and Lazarus after his return from the grave. With what a human interest does the poet clothe the familiar story! How reverently and yet with what natural and simple pathos does he touch upon the more intimate relations of the three persons who are the chief actors! The question which has come a thousand times to everyone who has lost a dear friend—the question whether love survives in the other world, whether those who have gone before miss those who are left behind and have any knowledge of their grief—this is the suggestion which brings the story home to us and makes it seem real and living.
—II, 258.

18. *In the temple*

O God, make of us what thou wilt;
  Guide thou the labor of our hand;
Let all our work be surely built
  As thou, the architect, hast planned;
But whatsoe'er thy power shall make
Of these frail lives, do not forsake
Thy dwelling. Let thy presence rest
Forever in the temple of our breast.
—IX, 87.

NOVEMBER

19. *Immortal Book*

True lovers of the Bible have an interest in all the elements of its life as an immortal book. They wish to discern, and rightly to appreciate, the method of its history, the spirit of its philosophy, the significance of its fiction, the power of its eloquence, and the charm of its poetry. They wish this all the more because they find in it something which is not in any other book: a vision of God, a hope for humanity, and an inspiration to righteousness, which are evidently divine.
—XV, 6.

20. *Asking for wisdom*

If God says to us, in the bright promise of youth, "Ask what I shall give thee," let us make the best choice, and answer, "Give me grace to know thy Son, the Christ, and to grow like him: for that is the true wisdom which leads to eternal life, and that is the true royalty which brings dominion over self, and that is the true happiness which flows unsought from fellowship with the Divine Life."
—IV, 165.

NOVEMBER

21. The source of authority

Christ is the light of all Scripture. Christ is the master of holy reason. Christ is the sole Lord and life of the true church. By his Word we test all doctrines, conclusions, and commands. On his Word we build all faith. This is *the* source of authority in the kingdom of heaven. Let us neither forget nor hesitate to appeal to it always with untrembling certainty and positive conviction.
—VII, 199.

22. Focused faith

To be sure of God, most wise, most mighty, most holy, most loving, our Father in heaven and on earth; to be sure of Christ, divine and human, our Brother and our Master, the pattern of excellence and the Redeemer from sin, the Savior of all who trust in him; to be sure of the Holy Spirit, the Comforter, the Guide, the Purifier, given to all who ask for him; to be sure of immortality, an endless life in which nothing can separate us from the love of God—let us concentrate our faith upon these things.
—IV, 231.

NOVEMBER

23. Rock of Ages

People have tried to lay other foundations, but they and their works have vanished. The bonfires have been kindled on a thousand hills, and have burned out. The floods have risen, and fallen, and swept away the frail edifices that have been built upon the sands of time. But the impregnable Rock remains unshaken, lifting all the lives that have been founded upon it high above the wrecks of ages, clearly outlined against the sky, like a crown of towers and a city that hath foundations, whose builder and maker is God.
—*IV, 238.*

24. Honest confession

How hard it is to confess that we have spoken without thinking, that we have talked nonsense! How many people say a thing in haste or in heat, without fully understanding or half meaning it, and then, because they have said it, hold fast to it, and try to defend it as if it were true! But how much wiser, how much more admirable and attractive, it is when people have the grace to perceive and acknowledge their mistakes! It gives us assurance that they are capable of learning, of growing, of improving, so that their future will be better than their past.
—*IV, 172*

NOVEMBER

25. *The ring of love*

But love also must move within the bounds of law, must be true to its vows. Not even the strongest and most beautiful soul may follow the guidance of passion without restraint; for the greater the genius, the beauty, the power, of those who transgress, the more fatal will be the influence of their sin upon other lives.
—II, 214.

26. *The source*

Behind every manifestation of spiritual life there is the Spirit. Behind Christianity there is Christ. Behind Christ there is God. For he is the brightness of the Father's glory, and the express image of his person; and the power that works in Christ, the power that has raised him from the dead and set him at God's right hand in heavenly places, is the power that is saving everyone that believeth, and reconciling the world to God. When we know that, despair ceases to exist, and joy fills the heart with music.
—IV, 94.

27. Unseen foundations

There are many noble principles and beautiful characters unconsciously built upon a Christian foundation, laid by a mother's prayers, a father's example, though the builder may not know or acknowledge it. Yes, there are even larger edifices, societies, nations, it may be, which are unconsciously based upon the moral ideal which is in Christ, and which silently acknowledge Christianity as the law of laws, even though God be not named in their constitution. They are like the villages in Egypt which were unwittingly erected upon the massive foundations of some ancient temple.
—*IV, 247.*

28. The love that leads life upward

There are many kinds of love, as many kinds
    of light,
And every kind of love makes a glory in
    the night.
There is love that stirs the heart, and love
    that gives it rest,
But the love that leads life upward is the
    noblest and the best.
—*IX, 52.*

NOVEMBER

29. Simple affairs

It would seem as if it ought to be the simplest affair in the world to lighten up a smudge. And so it is—if you are not trying.
—XIII, 218.

30. Holiday memories

But how close together are the fountains of grief and gladness! How often the flood of tears mingles with the stream of rejoicing! The festival which is all brightness to the young, brings to the old, memories of loss and sadness. Christmas and Thanksgiving Day, with all their merriment and laughter, awaken echoes in the house, in the heart, which whisper "Nevermore"; and the joy of the present seems to fade and grow dull compared with the joy that has departed. The past wins

"A glory from its being far,
   And orbs into the perfect star
   We saw not when we moved therein."
—I, 207.

DECEMBER

1. The gospel of selfishness

The privileged few are saying to their disciples that the world is a failure, humanity a mass of wretchedness, religion an outworn dream—the only refuge for the elect of wealth and culture is in art. Retreat into your gardens of pleasure. Let the plague take the city. Delight your eyes with all things fair and sweet. So shall it be well with you and your soul shall dwell at ease while the swine perish. It is the new gospel of pessimism which despairs of the common people because it despises them—nay, the old gospel of pessimism which seeks to secrete a selfish happiness in "the worst of all possible worlds." Nebuchadnezzar tried it in Babylon; Hadrian tried it in Rome; Solomon tried it in Jerusalem; and from all its palaces comes the same voice: *vanitas vanitatum et omnia vanitas.*

—II, 44.

2. The meaning and the story

"And now that his story is told, what does it mean?

How can I tell? What does life mean? If the meaning could be put into a sentence there would be no need of telling the story."
—*V, xii.*

3. Behind Nature

You tell me that it matters not whether the hand that guides the plow be pure and clean, or wicked and defiled. Nature feels alike and will do alike for both. I say, Not if God is behind Nature, not if Nature is the expression of his will. He may do alike, but he does not feel alike. As well say that he who made light and darkness cannot distinguish between them, as that he whose will is the moral law ever forgets it, ignores it, casts it aside, in any sphere or mode of his action. Evermore he loves the good, the true, the noble. Evermore he hates the base, the false, the evil. Evermore iniquity is an abomination unto him, and righteousness is his delight.
—*IV, 197.*

DECEMBER

4. Visions for guidance

We are on a path which leads upward, by sure and steady steps, when we begin to look at our future selves with eyes of noble hope and clear purpose, and see our figures climbing, with patient, dauntless effort, towards the heights of true manhood and womanhood. Visions like these are Joseph's dreams. They are stars for guidance. They are sheaves of promise. The very memory of them, if we cherish it, is a power of pure restraint and generous inspiration.
—VIII, 30.

5. The moment we see

The moment we see God behind the face of Nature—the moment we believe that this vast and marvellous procession of seasons and causes and changes, this array of interworking forces, is directed and controlled by a supreme, omniscient Holy Spirit, whose will is manifest in the springing of the seed, the ripening of the fruit, the fading of the leaf, the shining of the sun, and the falling of the rain—we cannot think that God is indifferent. It cannot be that he cares not whether the dwellers upon his earth are wicked or righteous, foul or pure, selfish or generous.
—IV, 196.

DECEMBER

6. Sure of two things

To see Christ as the true Son of God and the brother of all humanity, is to be sure that the soul is free, and that God is good.
—*VII, xvi.*

7. The seat of revelation

The seat of the divine revelation and the center of the divine atonement was and is the human life of God.
—*VII, 149.*

8. Called to fight

But out yonder in the wide forest, who knows what storms are raving tonight in the hearts of men, though all the woods are still? Who knows what haunts of wrath and cruelty and fear are closed tonight against the advent of the Prince of Peace? And shall I tell you what religion means to those who are called and chosen to dare and to fight, and to conquer the world for Christ? It means to launch out into the deep. It means to go against the strongholds of the adversary. It means to struggle to win an entrance for their Master everywhere.
—*X, 17.*

DECEMBER

9. A difference in good deeds

Here are two women going down to work among the sick and the poor. One goes because there is a fashion of it, because she would fain have the credit which belongs to the lady bountiful. She moves among them like an iceberg, and they hate her. She brings a chill with her which all her coals and blankets can never warm away. The other goes because she believes in it, believes that God wants her to do it, believes that the sorrowful and the distressed are Christ's brethren, and that she is bound to them, and that they have immortal souls which she may win for him. She moves among them like a sister of Jesus and friend of God; and of her the Master says, "Inasmuch as she hath done it unto one of the least of these my brethren, she hath done it unto me."
—IV, 46.

10. Into wiser hands

For what is it that faith does with these lives of ours? It just takes them up out of our weak, trembling, uncertain control and puts them into the hands of God. It makes them a part of his great plan. It binds them fast to his pure and loving will, and fills them with his life.
—IV, 131.

DECEMBER

11. *Gospel of the heavy-laden*

Hear the Master's risen word!
  Delving spades have set it free—
  Wake! the world has need of thee—
Rise, and let thy voice be heard,
Like a fountain disinterred,
  Upward springing, singing, sparkling;
  Through the doubtful shadows darkling;
  Till the clouds of pain and rage
  Brooding o'er the toiling age,
As with rifts of light are stirred
By the music of the Word;
Gospel for the heavy-laden,
  answer to the laborer's cry;
"Raise the stone, and thou shalt find Me:
cleave the wood, and there am I."
  —XIV, 5.

12. *The joy of trust*

Is there anything that pleases you more than to be trusted—to have even a little child look up into your face, and put out its hand to meet yours, and come to you confidingly? By so much as God is better than you are, by so much more does he love to be trusted. . . . There is a hand stretched out to you—a hand with a wound in the palm of it. Reach out the hand of your faith to clasp it, and cling to it, for without faith it is impossible to please God.

  —IV, 48.

DECEMBER

13. Slumber so deep

There is a slumber so deep that it annihilates time. It is like a fragment of eternity. Beneath its enchantment of vacancy, a day seems like a thousand years, and a thousand years might well pass as one day.
—XI, 31.

14. Unveiling glory

The humanity of Jesus was not the veiling but the unveiling of the divine glory. The limitations, temptations, and sufferings of manhood were the conditions under which alone Christ could accomplish the greatest work of the Deity—the redemption of a sinful race.
—VII, 149.

15. Pain, a proof of life

The sense of sin is not by any means a hopeless thing. It is an evidence of life, in its very pain; of enlightenment, in its very shame; of nearness to God in its very humiliation before him.
—XII, 34.

DECEMBER

16. The instinct of prayer

We must ask if we would receive, we must seek if we would find. We must knock if we desire to have the door of heaven opened to us.

Prayer is something that no one can understand; there is a mystery about it. We cannot explain how the voice of a mortal creature should have any influence upon the immortal God; how there should be any connection between the supplications which are wrung from our hearts by the pressure of want and danger and the fulfillment of those vast designs which have been formed from all eternity. But however that may be, prayer is an instinct of the human heart, and the religion which did not provide for it would be no religion at all.
—I, 198.

17. The inward kingdom

The kingdom of God which Jesus proclaims and establishes is a kingdom of the soul. Its deepest meaning is a personal experience. Its essence is righteousness and peace and joy in the Holy Ghost. Its dwelling place and seat of power is in the inner life.
—XII, 95.

DECEMBER

18. The steadiness of God

> "Why art thou cast down, O my soul?
> And why art thou disquieted within me?
> Hope thou in God: for I shall yet
> praise him,
> Who is the health of my countenance and
> my God."

Thy feelings will ebb and flow; thy heart will grow warm in summer's glow and cold in winter's chill; thou wilt be brave and steadfast today, downcast and anxious tomorrow; thy streams will be full in the rainy season, and in the time of drought they will be bare beds of stone. Turn away from thyself. Hope in God. He fainteth not, neither is he weary. He is the unfailing fountain; his affections do not decay; with him is no variableness, neither shadow of turning. When thou art dismayed, he is still full of an eternal peace. When thou art downcast, he is still untroubled.
—I, 169.

DECEMBER

19. The church for the world

Religion is for humanity. The church is for the world. Her mission will be fulfilled, not when she separates herself in lonely rapture from the doom of the race, and rises into a remote and selfish heaven, but when she draws the whole world with her into the light of God, and the knowledge of the Lord covers the earth as the waters cover the sea.
—I, 63.

20. Songs of deliverance

> "Thou art my hiding place; Thou wilt preserve me from trouble.
> Thou wilt compass me about with songs of deliverance."

There is a peculiar beauty in this last phrase. It suggests the picture of a company of singing angels joining hands about the son that was lost and found, and making him the center of a circle of joy. He is encompassed with songs; they are his guard, his defense. Music is like a wall round about him. Holy gladness is a secure protection to the soul. If any one is merry, let him sing psalms; and the little devils who are always to spoil every pure enjoyment, and to make every pleasure an occasion to sin, will fly away, like bats from a cavern when a torch is kindled.
—I, 93.

DECEMBER

21. *Called to quietness*

"Look you, my friends," said Winfried, "how sweet and peaceful is this convent tonight, on the eve of the nativity of the Prince of Peace! It is a garden full of flowers in the heart of winter; a nest among the branches of a great tree shaken by the winds; a still haven on the edge of a tempestuous sea. And this is what religion means for those who are chosen and called to quietude and prayer and meditation."
—X, 16.

22. *Another festival*

Christmas is truly the festival of childhood; but it should also be the festival of motherhood, for the child, even the holiest, is not divided from the mother. We may learn to think of infancy as sacred in the light that flows from the manger-cradle of Jesus. Yet it seems to me we cannot receive that truth perfectly unless we first learn to think of motherhood in the memory of her who found favor with God to receive and guard and cherish the Son of the Highest.
—III, 43.

23. Great joy

Joy is essential to true religion. A gloomy religion is far from God. A sad gospel is a contradiction in terms, like a black sun. "Behold," said the angel, "I bring you good tidings of great joy which shall be to all people." And that message was simply the news of a great power which had appeared in the world for salvation.
—IV, 93.

24. The first Christmas tree

"And here," said he, as his eyes fell on a young fir tree, standing straight and green, with its top pointing towards the stars, amid the divided ruins of the fallen oak, "here is the living tree, with no stain of blood upon it, that shall be the sign of your new worship. See how it points to the sky. Let us call it the tree of the Christ-child. Take it up and carry it to the chieftain's hall. You shall go no more into the shadows of the forest to keep your feasts with secret rites of shame. You shall keep them at home, with laughter and song and rites of love. The thunder-oak has fallen, and I think the day is coming when there shall not be a home in all Germany where the children are not gathered around the green fir tree to rejoice in the birth-night of Christ."
—X, 72.

DECEMBER

25. Christmas

Could every time-worn heart but see Thee
   once again,
A happy human child, among the homes
   of men,
The age of doubt would pass—the vision of
   Thy face
Would silently restore the childhood of
   the race.
—*IX, 59.*

26. Anno Domini

The birth of Jesus is the sunrise of the Bible. Towards this point the aspirations of the prophets and the poems of the psalmists were directed as the heads of flowers are turned towards the dawn. From this point a new day began to flow very silently over the world—a day of faith and freedom, a day of hope and love. When we remember the high meaning that has come into human life and the clear light that has flooded softly down from the manger-cradle in Bethlehem of Judea, we do not wonder that humanity has learned to reckon history from the birthday of Jesus, and to date all events by the years before or after the nativity of Christ.
—*III, 47.*

DECEMBER

27. God's philanthropy

Modern art, splendidly equipped and full of skill, waits for an inspiration to use its powers nobly. Modern beneficence, practical and energetic, lacks too often the ideal touch, the sense of beauty. Both these priceless gifts, and who can tell how many more, may be received again when the heart of our doubting age, still cherishing a deep love of faith and a strong belief in love, comes back to kneel at the manger-cradle where a little babe reveals the philanthropy of God.
—III, x.

28. The Other Wise Man

"You know the story of the Three Wise Men of the East, and how they travelled from far away to offer their gifts at the manger-cradle in Bethlehem. But have you ever heard the story of the Other Wise Man, who also saw the star in its rising, and set out to follow it, yet did not arrive with his brethren in the presence of the young child Jesus? Of the great desire of this fourth pilgrim, and how it was denied, yet accomplished in the denial; of his many wanderings and the probations of his soul; of the long way of his seeking, and the strange way of his finding, the One whom he sought—I would tell the tale as I heard the fragments of it in the Hall of Dreams, in the palace of the Heart of Man."
—V, xv.

DECEMBER

29. Jesus in Egypt

Thou wayfaring Jesus, a pilgrim and stranger,
    Exiled from heaven by love at thy birth,
Exiled again from thy rest in the manger,
    A fugitive child 'mid the perils of earth—
Cheer with thy fellowship all who are weary,
    Wandering far from the land they love;
Guide every heart that is homeless and dreary,
    Safe to its home in thy presence above.
    —IX, 59.

30. The ship and the tide

The day is coming when the great ship of the world, guided by the hand of the Son of God, shall float out of the clouds and storms, out of the shadows and conflicts, into the perfect light of love, and God shall be all in all. The tide that bears the world to that glorious end is the sovereignty of God.
    —VII, 279.

DECEMBER

31. *A benediction*

There seems to be a natural instinct which makes us desire that every religious service should end with a blessing. For nothing is more grateful and quieting to the heart than "the benediction / That follows after prayer."

After this old fashion would I close my book. The faces of my readers are unknown to me, even as the pilgrims who called through the darkness were unknown to the watchmen upon the Temple walls. But whoever you are, at least a benediction shall go after you. Your life is a pilgrimage. May mercy follow you out of Zion, and peace bring you to your home!

—*I, 259.*